VOODOO DEFICITS

Robert Ortner

DOW JONES-IRWIN
Homewood, Illinois 60430

This publication is designed to provide accurate and
authoritative information in regard to the subject matter
covered. It is sold with the understanding that the
publisher is not engaged in rendering legal, accounting, or
other professional service. If legal advice or other expert
assistance is required, the services of a competent
professional person should be sought.

*From a Declaration of Principles jointly adopted by a Committee
of the American Bar Association and a Committee of Publishers.*

Sponsoring editor: Jeffrey A. Krames
Project editor: Jane Lightell
Production manager: Diane Palmer
Jacket design: Image House
Compositor: Carlisle Communications, Ltd.
Typeface: 11/13 Century Schoolbook
Printer: Arcata Graphics/Kingsport

Library of Congress Cataloging-in-Publication Data

Ortner, Robert.
    Voodoo deficits / Robert Ortner.
      p.   cm.
    ISBN 1-55623-280-2
    1. United States—Economic policy—1981– 2. Supply-side
economics—United States. 3. Budget deficits—United States.
4. Balance of trade—United States. 5. United States—Foreign
economic relations. 6. Competition, International. I. Title.
HC106.8.O78 1990
339.5'23'0973—dc20   90–30834
                                         CIP

To Evelyn, Peter, and Nicole
for a beautiful life

PREFACE

During the 1970s and early 1980s, the American economy and the American people suffered through their most difficult time since the depression of the 1930s. Huge increases in oil prices forced Americans to transfer literally hundreds of billions of dollars of their income and wealth to OPEC and other oil producers. Much of our capital equipment, normally run by plentiful energy, was made obsolete. Economic growth slowed to a crawl. Perhaps it is amazing that we managed to grow at all. One unfortunate consequence was that the unemployment rate rose to its highest level since 1941.

By 1982, with the aid of some stringent monetary policy, inflation subsided to what has come to be regarded as moderate proportions; that, at least, lowered one barrier to growth. The Reagan administration then gave the economy a new shot of adrenalin through tax cuts. The economy rebounded smartly and continued growing strongly through 1988. The expansion carried with it rising employment, incomes, and standards of living. By the end of 1988, the economy approached a full employment level of operations.

The political opposition—including politicians and economists—worked hard to convince the public that the economic gains were imaginary or soon would be confiscated somehow. But the public did not buy the story—certainly not in 1984 or in 1988—because the critics' facts were wrong, and because some of the arguments did not even make sense.

Nonetheless, the rhetoric managed to achieve something else—a new economic mythology in the manner of George Orwell's "Newspeak." Among these myths, you will find, for example, that higher government spending and lower taxes no longer stimulate the economy; they stifle it. You will also find that a growing trade deficit, which formerly meant that we were losing business to foreigners, now is good for us. Why? Because the money we pay to foreigners for their goods supposedly is financing our economy. These new interpretations of our domestic and foreign deficits have given them a "voodoo" character.

I had two basic purposes in writing this book. One was to explain why these statements are myths and why they are not today's problems. The other was to identify the genuine problems facing the United States in the coming years and indicate what to do about them. Despite the recovery and gains of the 1980s, the work is unfinished. The economy is in need of revitalization. Focusing on budget deficits, alleged dependence on foreign capital, and foreign debt will not produce the needed changes.

This book takes a minority—but not a unique—view of these issues, at least within the economics profession. I did not write it to satisfy my contrary personality. America is still the world's economic leader; but the other industrial countries— *all of them*—are gaining on us. At the turn of the century, we are likely to be in third place. Following the advice of the economic establishment will ensure that we will be third and heading downward in the standings. I, for one, do not care to see that happen—especially as it is not inevitable, and we can do better. This is not just a statistical race; it is our standard of living. Our citizens want and deserve better. Policies either in place or proposed through 1989 will not do the job.

The book is addressed to business people, investors, the general public interested in this subject, students of economics and related disciplines, and economists and politicians. I placed the last group last because politicians and some economists are close to hopeless—they will not be persuaded by anything I say or any facts I present. I am counting on the first few groups to tell the last group what it must do. That is what democracy is about anyway.

I have tried to present data and arguments so as to help readers make up their own minds about what our problems are and what to do about them. Some economists will attack my arguments. That, in itself, will not mean that I am wrong. Remember that these economists have vested interests in their past writings and statements. Please make up your own minds on the basis of what sounds right to you. If they tell you that you really do not understand what is happening or its future consequences, you should be particularly suspicious of them and their comments. Joan Robinson, the eminent British economist, observed that one purpose of studying economics is that you will not be deceived as easily by economists.

During my tenure at the Department of Commerce, I benefited greatly from stimulating discussions with my colleagues and from the wealth of information available through the department's statistical agencies, the Bureau of Economic Analysis and the Bureau of the Census. I do not know where the jokes began about government bureaucrats; they could not have originated at these agencies. Their staffs are highly dedicated, competent professionals. I was very happy to have the executive responsibility for these agencies and was honored to be associated with these people.

I owe special thanks to Carl Cox, Director of the Office of Economic Conditions in the Under Secretary's office. He read the first draft of my manuscript, listened patiently to my arguments, and made important suggestions regarding the material presented in this book. As I had already left office, it was on his own time—he no longer had to do it. But he is not responsible for errors that remain or for my views.

At the Commerce Department, I also benefited greatly from periodic briefings and assistance by Betty L. Barker, Chief, International Investment Division, and Robert P Parker, Associate Director for National Economic Accounts, both at the Bureau of Economic Analysis; and by Charles P Waite, Associate Director for Economic Programs at the Bureau of the Census. Since I left the department, they continue to offer advice and counsel when I call on them. None of them bears any responsibility for my views, for the selection of data included in this book, or for the manner of their presentation.

Several other people provided help in locating and organizing data that I needed. I am particularly grateful to Janet Norwood, Commissioner of Labor Statistics; to Edwin Dale, Counselor to the Director, Office of Management and Budget; and to George McKittrick and John Tschetter, senior economists in the Commerce Department's Office of Economic Conditions. Again, none of these individuals is responsible for my views or the manner of presenting this material.

The manuscript was typed with interest and care by Lisa Schworn, a student at Drew University, and by Catherine Coloff, during evening hours after full workdays at Exxon. Both of them delivered accurate finished products always on time.

My wife, Evelyn, a writer herself, and former Counselor to the Secretary of Health and Human Services, nourished, nurtured, tolerated, and encouraged me through this book. Despite a reasonable, healthy dislike and mistrust of economics, she read the manuscript and made numerous improvements in my presentation. She assures me that I have said little in this book that I have not "been saying over the years." I am not absolutely certain what she means by that, but I took it as a compliment.

Robert Ortner

CONTENTS

Introduction

A LITTLE BACKGROUND MUSIC

Myth: The end is nigh.
Fact: Science will continue to push back
the horizons. No end is in sight.

Almost two hundred years ago, the Reverend Thomas R. Malthus warned that continued population growth would quickly absorb the world's limited food supplies. As a result, he believed that mankind faced two dire consequences: an ever declining standard of living as less and less productive land is brought into use (economists' famous law of diminishing returns), and a grinding limit to population itself at or near starvation conditions. This description of mankind's fate so impressed the historian Thomas Carlyle that he named economics a "dismal science."

However, Carlyle did not refute Malthus's analysis, which was logical, reasonable, perhaps obvious, and wrong. That is not intended as a criticism of Malthus. After all, how could he have foreseen the industrial revolution of the nineteenth century and the scientific explosion of the twentieth? How could he have predicted a slowing population growth even without the restrictions imposed by starvation? But isn't this what has always plagued forecasters? If only we could foresee new developments that alter trends.

An outstanding recent example of this inability occurred at the beginning of the 1970s, when we could not foresee OPEC oil embargoes that ushered in a new economic period. As late as 1972, only a year before the first embargo, our policymakers in Washington were still restricting oil imports

1

to support the domestic price in order to help our domestic producers!

One area in which we have made great progress is the development of mathematical equations, or so-called models, and their use on large-scale computers to perform analyses and prepare forecasts. These new tools can now complete in seconds and in much greater detail projections that formerly required weeks or even months. However, models and computers still project on the basis of past trends. Altering those trends in preparing forecasts still requires the intervention of human judgment.

Undaunted, unimpressed, and apparently uninfluenced by our technological progress, a group of 30 individuals from a number of countries met in Rome in 1968 to reconsider, presumably in a more scientific way than Malthus, mankind's economic circumstances and prospects. The group became the now famous "Club of Rome." Eventually, they may be infamous.

They broadened the scope of Malthus's analysis to cover a variety of natural resources. They developed elaborate mathematical models and ran them through computers. Their conclusion? If current trends of population growth and resource depletion continue, our limits to growth on this planet will be reached within 100 years, followed by an abrupt decline in population and economic activity as the world's population reaches the end of its tether.

The Club will be just as wrong as Malthus was and for the same reason—the basic fallacy of projecting currently known supplies of materials and current knowledge indefinitely into the future. The application of mathematics and computers clothe the analysis in respectability but not necessarily in accuracy. The results are no better than the starting assumptions. And computers are not discriminating. They will process any data fed to them—"garbage in, garbage out," as they say.

Toward the end of the 1980s, a few scientists began to claim new breakthroughs in nuclear fusion and in superconductivity. Others argued that the claims were, at best, premature. Perhaps neither is around the corner. However, if either of these developments is commercially feasible in a hundred years, it would give the world's economy another quantum boost. Although no one can predict the exact nature of scientific discoveries and breakthroughs, there is no doubt that technological progress will continue.

The Club's conclusions, however, are not just interesting or curious analyses. They are far more dangerous than those of Malthus. Malthus's views were descriptive; the Club's are prescriptive—that is, they include recommendations to slow technical and industrial development. Capital plant, they say, should be held constant and investment kept to a minimum. But these are the very things we need to improve people's standards of living and cure or relieve many of the ills the Club members complained about. Malthus and the members of the Club of Rome were wrong because they underestimated scientific progress; in addition, they did not foresee the power of technology or real capital (plant and equipment), which were instrumental in widening the economic horizons.

It is interesting to note that agriculture, which was originally believed to be mankind's ultimate bottleneck, is now rarely mentioned as a limit to growth. On the contrary, with more land brought under cultivation, and with the application of fertilizers and mechanization, our capacity to produce foodstuffs has grown much faster than consumption. Today our agricultural problems and issues concern limiting—rather than limited—production and supporting market prices that are weak because of *excess* output.

Under strong political pressure, many countries maintain programs to subsidize exports in order to sell off their surpluses and limit imports to protect their farmers. In 1986, the U.S. government spent about $30 billion on what it calls Farm Income Stabilization.[1] Government aid to farmers fell to about $15 billion in fiscal years 1988 and 1989 because 1988's drought cut production and raised market prices. The Administration currently is projecting further declines in these outlays, but the amount of future reductions will depend both on market conditions and political demands.

---

[1]*Budget of the United States Government, Fiscal Year 1990.* Keep this in mind when considering the budget deficit and what to do about it.

Agriculture may not be a problem now, but energy— especially oil—some argue, is another matter. Supplies are finite and, therefore, will run out eventually. It is difficult to argue with that logic, but one may reasonably ask when. New supplies are continually being found, even though at higher costs of development.

There are also alternative competing fuels in abundant quantities, especially natural gas. One *New York Times* report pointed out that natural gas available to continued drilling may amount to as much as a 5,000-year supply, plus a 1,600-year supply from coal gasification.[2] We already know how to separate hydrogen from water. That is a simple procedure. The only question is cost, which is declining. Our cars can run on hydrogen, which is in virtually unlimited supply and has the added advantage of not polluting the atmosphere.

Another *New York Times* article began with the headline "An Energy Glut . . ." and observed that known reserves of oil, gas, and coal are rising faster than consumption. "It's not just oil; reserves of coal are up 80 percent in three years."[3]

Despite the protests of sandwich-board doomsayers, mankind is not approaching the end of its tether. In reality, only a relatively small portion of the tether has been reeled out to date. Maybe there is no tether.

But doomsayers do not give up. Now a new breed of economists, focusing on financial analysis, are arguing that the economy is in dire straits because of financial strains and limitations. Their argument is that large federal deficits and borrowing "absorb" private saving, crowd out private investment, and inhibit economic growth. But are they correct? What do the facts show? In 1982, government borrowing—by their accounting—nearly equaled private saving; that is, it "absorbed" nearly all private saving. Supposedly, we had inadequate saving. Yet 1983 and 1984 were years of extraordinarily strong economic growth, including large increases in

---

[2]*New York Times*, "Professor Backs Natural Gas for Autos" June 4, 1989, p. 10.
[3]*New York Times*, "Ideas & Trends", October 15, 1989, p. 65.

investment. Obviously, something is wrong with their system of analysis.

For one thing, an active, purposeful rise in the budget deficit stimulates the economy. It does not depress it. Increased government spending adds directly to economic activity, while tax cuts add indirectly through higher consumer and/or business spending. The economy was in recession in 1982 because we had too little *spending,* not because we had too little *saving.*

For another, private saving out of current income greatly understates the sources of funds available to finance economic growth. Ultimately, the amount of credit is controlled by the Federal Reserve Board whose goal essentially is to promote high levels of employment and economic activity without accelerating inflation.

This explains why credit was readily available in 1983 and 1984 when we had high unemployment and large amounts of idle plant capacity but was tightening in 1988 and 1989. It is nonsense to argue that the economy cannot grow when 10 percent of the labor force is unemployed and only 70 percent of industrial capacity is in use. Furthermore, government policies to restrict growth in the face of that much idle capacity would be ridiculous. The only legitimate long term limits to our growth are technology and physical capacity. If *finance* is the actual limiting factor, we need new managers in Washington.

The proper focus of economic policy is the real economy. By *real economy,* I mean the fundamental economic factors of physical output, jobs, and the purchasing power of individuals' incomes. This should not be confused with economics data measured in current prices, including inflation. For example, if personal incomes were to rise, say, 5 percent this year from last, and retail prices also rose 5 percent, we would be no better off in terms of real purchasing power than we were last year. Income adjusted for inflation, or "real income," would be unchanged.

Charts I-1 and I-2 show our progress since World War II in some of the most important measures of economic activity. These include real consumer spending, which depends mainly

CHART I–1
Disposable Income and Consumption per Capita (In Thousands of 1982 dollars)

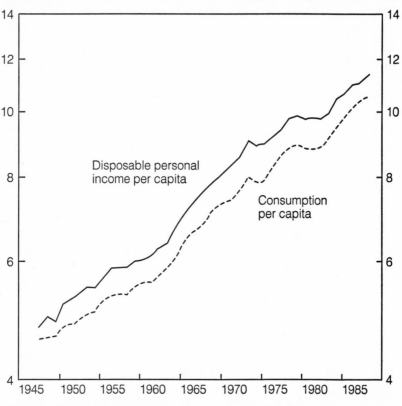

Source: Bureau of Economic Analysis

on real disposable personal income—that is, income after taxes and after price changes. This depends, in turn, on overall economic growth, which depends on growth in productivity (output per worker per hour), which depends on technical progress and on growth in capital stock (plant and equipment) per worker. And there you have it, the economy and our standards of living almost in a nutshell.

Obviously, economic problems, analyses, policies, and progress involve many other factors. But when it comes to growth, standards of living, and competitiveness, the key factors are technical progress and real, or physical, capital

CHART I–2
Output/Labor and Capital/Labor Ratios, Business Sector (1977 = 100)

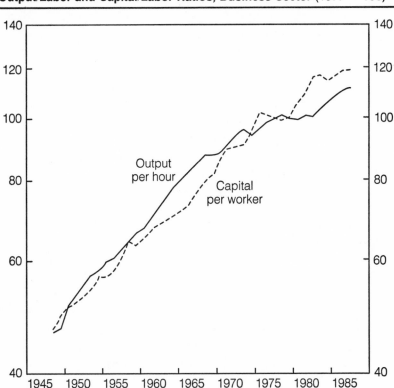

Source: Bureau of Economic Analysis and Bureau of Labor Statistics

investment. These are the factors that enable us to improve
both the quality and efficiency of productive equipment and
raise both the quality and the quantity of goods available to
consumers.

For many years, economics professors and textbooks have
been instructing students that economics is the study of
allocating scarce resources among competing uses. Scarce not
in the sense of unavailable at any price, but available with
enough limitation so that the resources, or goods, will command some market price. Thus, choice is at the heart of
economic analysis and policymaking. Choice for individual
consumers might involve a second VCR versus a third television set. In the context of the subject matter contained in

these charts, it might also involve a choice between more consumption now and giving up a present increase in favor of more investment in capital equipment. This would lead to faster economic growth and still higher levels of income and consumption in the future.

This kind of choice is more critical now that our economy is relatively fully employed than it was in 1982 when we had considerable idle resources of both labor and industrial capacity. Then we were able to raise the output of almost everything—consumption, housing, defense, *and* investment. This is not really possible in 1990. Now, we face genuine choices, and our first priority should be more capital investment.

Those who argue that we should raise taxes to reduce the federal budget deficit and thereby free up government resources for private use are misleading the public. Government borrowing does not use up real economic resources. Government activity, or spending, does. Federal spending now amounts to almost 23 percent of gross national product (GNP), up from about 19 percent 20 to 25 years ago. Higher taxes would not shrink the government's use of resources; in reality, they would encourage government to spend more. If that happens, it would cut into consumer resources and standards of living and cut into business investment just when we need more.

That is not to say that government borrowing has no effect on the private economy. It does. It affects the capital markets and interest rates. Therefore, it has an indirect effect on interest-sensitive sectors of the economy, such as home-building. How much of an effect depends on the growth in government borrowing and on Federal Reserve policy in supplying credit to the market. The Fed's policy, in turn, depends on the state of the economy. They will provide and accommodate more rapid growth in credit during times of high unemployment (1982) than in times of low unemployment (1990). Thus, we come back to the real economy and the availability of real resources.

At this economic juncture, government policymakers, legislative and executive, can contribute to economic well-being and U.S. competitiveness by cutting spending or at least holding the line on spending. This would free up resources for more capital investment and technical development. But just making resources available through less government or consumer spending (that is, more saving) is not enough. The resources must be pointed in the right directions—*and used.* Absence may make the heart grow fonder (or is it absinthe?), but not abstinence. Nor does abstinence from spending make the economy stronger. We must move quickly to remove fiscal disincentives for business investment and for research and development (R & D) and begin to *encourage* these activities.

The encouragement must come from fiscal measures such as investment and R & D tax credits. Monetary policy cannot do this job because it is too blunt an instrument. Further monetary stimulation at this time would boost homebuilding and consumer spending more than capital investment. It would boost inflation as well.

Investment and technical development are the fields on which the international competitive battles ultimately will be won and lost. In these comments, I am not laying claim to any great discovery or important originality. They are common sense—which, of course, does not mean that our elected officials will translate them into policy actions of their own volition.

"Classical" economists wrote of the importance of technology and investment many years ago. For example, about 70 years ago, Alfred Marshall, one of the giants of the field, wrote that

> The growth of the national dividend depends on the continued progress of invention and the accumulation of expensive appliances for production. . . . Nearly all of the innumerable inventions that have given us our command over nature have been made by independent workers; . . . contributions from government officials all the world over have been relatively small.[4]

"The more things change, . . ."

Today, the United States is frequently referred to as a second-rate economic power. To the extent that this is true, it

---

[4]Alfred Marshall, *Principles of Economics,* 8th ed. (New York: MacMillan, 1920), p. 712. Similarly, p. 304.

is because of our relatively poor performance in research and development and in capital investment. And if this performance is poor, it is largely because our governmental policies discourage these activities. Our so-called twin deficits—budget and foreign trade—are consequences, not causes, of our competitive position in the world.

Chapter One

IS THE UNITED STATES BACK IN THE MINOR LEAGUES?

Myth: The United States has lost its
economic lead.
Fact: We are really still number one,
but . . .

The short answer: No! Not only are we still in the "majors," we are actually still in first place. Then why do so many people think we are second-rate? For example, a *Business Month* article recently reported that only 22 percent of those responding to an opinion survey thought that the United States is the top economic power today and that "34 percent believe America has less economic power than Japan or West Germany."[1]

Since this perception is mistaken, what is the source of the misinformation? I believe it is mainly a steady flow of criticism, essentially political, widely quoted, and frequently supported by the press. These criticisms usually originate in Washington. And in Washington where one stands depends on where one sits. Especially if one sits on the opposition side of the political aisle.

The criticism usually attributes America's economic demise to our trade and/or federal budget deficits. After all, Germany and Japan have trade surpluses; so America, living "in the red," so to speak, is surely behind them. However, a number of less developed countries (LDCs) also have trade

---

[1]Leonard Silk, "The Kindest Cuts and the Least Painful Increases," *Business Month,* February 1989, p. 9.

surpluses. And these are countries struggling to pay interest on foreign debts and to maintain minimum subsistence for their populations. Obviously, this is a "voodoo" argument, more smoke and mirrors than economic reality.

In recent years, trade surpluses have been reported not only by Germany and Japan, but by Botswana, Gabon, Malaysia, Hungary, Poland, Argentina, Chile, Colombia, Mexico, Surinam, Uruguay, and Venezuela among others. Are they all greater economic powers than the United States? In many of these countries, despite already depressed living standards, they have had to suppress their economies in order to reduce imports to accumulate foreign exchange to service external debts. That is hardly a sign of strength. No, the trade balance alone is certainly not proof of economic strength.

Nor are we alone among industrial nations in generating federal budget deficits. In 1988, Canada, Japan, France, Germany, and Italy also had budget deficits. The United Kingdom reported a surplus, but their trade balance remained in deficit. I point out these facts also to refute the comment repeated ad nauseam that trade and budget deficits go hand in hand.

So what do these trade and budget balances demonstrate? Not much. And for the United States, these balances are a relatively insignificant part of the economy. The warnings about how our budget deficits are mortgaging our future fall somewhere between greatly exaggerated and irrelevant.

The question here concerns economic power, and that is a much broader concept than foreign trade and budgets. To begin, the U.S. population now totals some 250 million people. Japan's population is roughly half that of the United States. As for France, West Germany, Italy, and the United Kingdom, each has about a quarter of our population. Similarly, the number of people employed in the United States now totals about 120 million. Japan's workforce is approximately half the size of America's, and the other countries' are about one fifth the size of ours. Moreover, since the U.S. business expansion began in late 1982, we have added almost 20 million people to our payrolls; these five countries combined have added fewer than five million, and those are mainly in

Japan and England. Since 1982, most of those economies have not been very robust.

Of course population alone, like deficits, does not signify economic power. We need only to look at the population masses and economic messes in Russia and China to know this is true. Instead, we need to consider what these populations produce. A country's gross domestic product (GDP) is a comprehensive measure of its output. However, an international comparison of output is complicated by the fact that each country measures these values in its own currency, and exchange rates fluctuate widely in the marketplace.

In 1988, Japan's GDP totaled 364 trillion yen, and West Germany's 2.1 trillion deutsche marks. How much are these worth in dollars? At what exchange rate for the dollar? The dollar reached its latest peak in early 1985. By late 1987, it had fallen roughly 50 percent against the other major currencies. From the end of 1987 to mid-1989, the dollar rose about 15 percent, and then fell about 5 percent by the end of the year. Thus, comparing the United States' GDP with other countries' output meaningfully and consistently can be difficult.

Moreover, inflation rates differ among these countries. An increase in the value of output because of higher prices is not a genuine or "real" gain. Therefore, adjustments must be made for inflation as well.

The Organization for Economic Cooperation and Development (OECD), a Paris-based international group for research and policy development, has conducted considerable research in this area. It has developed what are called "purchasing power parity" (PPP) exchange rates. These rates are independent of market exchange rates. The PPP rates are based on general price levels in each country and are calculated so that a dollar can buy the same physical quantity of goods in Tokyo, Bonn, Paris, London, or Rome as in Washington. PPP exchange rates may shift over time because of differing inflation rates among these countries but are independent of market fluctuations.

Using these rates, the Bureau of Labor Statistics (BLS), U.S. Department of Labor, shows some interesting relative values.[2] In 1988, Canada's GDP was only 10 percent of the United States', that is, 90 percent less; Japan's was 36 percent of the United States'; Germany's 18 percent; and France's, Italy's, and the United Kingdom's each about 16 percent. As I said previously, in sheer, aggregate economic output, the United States is number one, and by a wide margin.

Aggregate national output, however, is not a meaningful indicator of each country's economic well-being. Of course our output is largest—our population is largest by far. If our output were not largest, we would be a sorry lot indeed.

On a per capita basis, the differences in output are much narrower, but the United States is still number one. Among the other major countries, Canada comes closest to the United States, with GDP per capita at about 94 percent of ours. Then Japan at 73 percent, followed by Germany at 72 percent, France at 70 percent, and Italy and the United Kingdom each at about 67 percent.[3]

Our total output (measured by GDP) is what produces our incomes or livelihoods; but even on a per capita basis, it is not the only measure of our well-being. We can employ a variety of measures to quantify standards of living, but these vary from country to country due to differing tastes and customs. Furthermore, quantitative measures cannot fully describe a country's quality of life.

Along with the highest level of output and incomes per capita, U.S. residents enjoy the highest consumption levels among the major industrial countries. But variations among countries and consumption categories are also interesting. On a per capita basis, the French and Italians eat more than we do. The French and West Germans drink more alcoholic beverages, as do the Canadians; the Italians drink less. The British consume less of both. We generally spend more in several other areas including clothing, fuel, housing (except as com-

---

[2]*Comparative Real Gross Domestic Product, Real GDP Per Capita . . . , 1950–1988,* prepared by the U.S. Department of Labor, Bureau of Labor Statistics, Office of Productivity and Technology, August 1989.
[3]Ibid., June 1989.

pared to the Japanese), and education (except as compared to the Canadians). On a per capita basis, we have more cars, telephones, and television sets.

The TV category may not be entirely a blessing. Perhaps we would be a more learned society if we read more and watched television less. We also consume more cigarettes per capita. The French and Germans spend as much as we do on medical care in general and much more on pharmaceutical products. Unfortunately, we also have the highest infant mortality rate (except for Italy, which has about the same rate that we do).

Obviously, in a few areas we should and can improve our performance. But, overall, our record is tops. Perhaps these comments overemphasize consumption. Economists generally use consumption as a basic measure of standards of living. I prefer to use income for that purpose. I referred earlier to real disposable personal income, that is income after taxes and after inflation. This is our best single measure of individuals' basic purchasing power.

If our policymakers in Washington ever gain the good sense to reduce consumption incentives and raise incentives for investment, consumption would slow temporarily and investment would rise. This transition surely would not be a sign of a lower standard of living. Individuals' incomes would grow more rapidly because of increased investment and would accommodate still higher consumption levels in the future.

So what's the problem? Unfortunately, there is a problem and it is economic growth. Leroy "Satchel" Paige, legendary baseball pitcher, once explained his philosophy of life: "Don't look back, they may be gaining on you." And when asked for the secret of his extraordinary longevity as an athlete, he reportedly answered that he ate nothing but fried foods, because fried foods "angry up the blood."

The long answer to the question in our chapter heading: We are number one in the "majors" now, but nearly all our competitors are gaining on us. The BLS data show that over a 28-year period, 1960 to 1988, all of these countries achieved as fast or faster growth in GDP per capita than we did. The years 1960 and 1988 provide useful comparisons for the United

States in that the unemployment rates were similar—about 5.5 percent. The economy, therefore, was at about the same point in the business cycle; and change during the period represents a long-term trend rather than a business cycle or parts of cycles.

From 1960 to 1988, U.S. GDP per capita grew an average of 2.1 percent per year, as did British output. The German economy grew 2.7 percent per year; the Canadian and French, 3 percent; the Italian, 3.5 percent; and the Japanese, 5.5 percent. Everyone knows about the Japanese economic "miracle," but what about the Italian? I can recall wondering some years ago how they could continue to perform so well when their government fell nearly every year. Then it occurred to me that one reason for their excellent performance was that their government was not there to interfere.

These countries' levels of output in 1988 suggest a startling fact: If their growth rates continue, Canada's output per capita will be on a par with that of the United States in about five and a half years, and Japan's in about nine and a half years.

Actually, relative growth improved in the United States after 1982. During the ensuing six years, only Canada and Japan gained slightly against the United States, while the other countries fell back. But let's not start the parade and fireworks just yet. From 1982 to 1988, the U.S. unemployment rate fell from over 10 percent to about 5.5 percent. That is, our somewhat improved relative performance was because of a cyclical expansion (we also have contractions). Cyclical expansions are temporary and do not promise the same performance over the long term.

Most economists agree that in 1989, the U.S. economy had reached full employment of its resources. What is meant by this is an unemployment level consistent with stable inflation. Growth will have to slow again to keep inflation from accelerating sharply. And this means that our growth probably will settle back to a level consistent with its long-term trend. If these other countries can sustain their growth trends, the United States will be running third in per capita output as it enters the next century. Canada will be second, and you-know-who will be first. Their standard of living will have passed ours and they will continue to widen the gap unless we take the steps necessary to "rev up" our economic engine.

But let's not hit the panic button either. Much of the fault lies in ourselves and we can improve our performance. Except for Canada, we are much more generously endowed with natural resources than are these other industrial countries, our trading partners and main competitors. Japan and Britain have similar economies, in that they import raw materials and convert them into finished goods for domestic consumption and reexport. Japan is good at it. The United Kingdom under Mrs. Thatcher has improved.

The United States emerged from World War II with its industrial base not only intact, but enhanced by its all-out war efforts. The others, with the exception of Canada, were in shambles. Rebuilding their economies was a long-term undertaking and offered an opportunity to employ the latest technologies, which were in large part developed here. This provided our allies, old and new, with some temporary benefit.

In sporting events, we are told that "playing catch-up ball" is difficult and usually unproductive because it means disrupting one's "game plan." But in economic development, it is both easy and productive. It means copying others' technology—without the costly research and development— and adapting it, or its desirable aspects, to one's own system. Not that this is a new idea. It was well-described by Thorsten Veblen many years ago,[4] and it is much more relevant today. Copying or applying technology developed elsewhere has become increasingly easy and is now potentially instantaneous with today's global communications systems.

This is not to say that we should lie back and watch everyone pass us by and then try to follow their leads. We can do better on our own, and we can do better *now*. Our industrial trading partners devote a larger share of their GDP than we do to research and development and even more to capital investment. As a result, they have achieved faster

---

[4]Thorsten Veblen, "On the Penalty of Taking the Lead," in *Imperial Germany and the Industrial Revolution*. Reprinted in *The Portable Veblen*, (New York: Viking Press, 1950), p. 364.

growth in productivity—that is, output per hour worked, than we have. And in this regard, our fault certainly lies in ourselves.

Using data from the manufacturing sector of the economy[5] and comparing our productivity growth against the same five countries during the same period, 1960 to 1988, the United States at 2.8 percent per year has compiled the *worst* record of all. Average productivity growth in Canada from 1960 to 1988 was 3.3 percent per annum; the United Kingdom, 3.7 percent; Germany, 4.4 percent; France, 4.9 percent; Italy, 5.5 percent; and Japan (are you ready?), 7.8 percent *per year.*

In mid-1989, the U.S. government under provisions of the 1988 Omnibus Trade and Competitiveness Act cited Japan, among several other nations, for unfairly restricting imports and thereby engaging in unfair trading practices. They do. I can remember some estimates made in the Commerce Department in the mid-1980s that Japan's import restrictions and obstacles cost the United States, or our manufacturers and farmers, to be more precise, as much as $15 billion a year in exports, perhaps more. But don't forget that our trade deficit with Japan alone is on the order of $50 billion, so that the complete removal of all of their trade barriers would not eliminate the deficit.

And don't forget, too, that we have our own import restrictions. For example, we maintain import quotas on cars. Of course, they are "voluntary" on Japan's part, but we pressured them to do it. We also restrict imports of steel and textiles. Senator Fritz Hollings once announced that "You can't go to war in a Japanese Uniform."[6] Why not, Fritz? If they make better uniforms and make them cheaper, we *should* buy them. His comment is simply a battle-cry for protectionism.

---

[5]Manufacturing data are relevant for two reasons: Our foreign trade and our competitiveness, or lack of it, are mainly in manufacturing; and we can measure productivity more accurately in manufacturing than in service industries. These data are from BLS Report No. 89–322, June 30, 1989.

[6]Robert Hershey "Reagan Selects Trade 'Strike Force,' " *New York Times,* October 3, 1985, p. D15.

In this, as in other areas, protection, other than for *genuine* national security reasons, always benefits a narrow constituency at the expense of the rest of the country. In the auto industry, for example, import restrictions raise the price of both imports and domestics. This is because exporters ship more high-priced models to the United States, and dealers can command higher markups. Furthermore, reduced competition permits domestic producers to raise their prices. In a study several years ago, Robert W. Crandall of the Brookings Institution estimated that these restrictions cost American consumers $4 billion per year. That amounts to $160,000 per year for each job saved.[7]

About 35 years ago, John Foster Dulles, then Secretary of State, sent a memorandum to President Eisenhower regarding a meeting with Premier Yoshida of Japan. Secretary Dulles reported that he had explained to the premier that Japan should not expect to export very much to the United States because Japan did not make the kinds or quality of goods that Americans wanted. In only three decades, the relationship has turned 180 degrees. *They* now tell *us* that, and to some extent they are right.

The point is that if all restrictions were removed on both sides, the U.S. deficit with Japan would not be eliminated. Part of it may be their unfair practices, but another part reflects their strong competitiveness. In a word, they're good. They concentrate on enlarging their economic pie. We seem to focus mainly on dividing ours up and do not seem to care whether our pie grows or not.

Competitiveness involves many things which I will discuss further in Chapter 6. But much of it can be summed up in a few factors: At the late 1989 exchange rate of 144 yen to the dollar, Japanese compensation costs in manufacturing were about 18 percent less than U.S. costs. This means that to improve our competitive position, the dollar must decline further relative to the yen, or our labor costs must rise more slowly than theirs do, or both.

---

[7]Hobart Rowan, "Get Rid of Auto Quotas," *Washington Post,* November 4, 1984, p. K1.

Another key factor is productivity. Productivity gains offset wage increases and contribute directly to cost competitiveness. And in this, Japan is not just world-class, they are the world record-holders. Productivity comes from a few sources. Among them, as I discussed earlier, are technological development and investment in new plant and equipment—bringing technical progress to the factory floor. We have done relatively poorly on both counts and especially poorly in capital investment.

Not only is Japan first in growth of output, but their products are top-notch in quality and style. For some years, *Consumer Reports* has given Japanese cars top ratings in frequency-of-repair records. It did not happen by chance alone. Quality must be designed into the product at the beginning of the process, and it must be a primary goal of management and production workers. If our auto companies had sufficient interest in producing quality products, we would not have to force consumers to buy domestic cars through import quota limits. Maybe what we need is more fried food in our diets to "angry up our blood" so that we can compete more effectively.

During the 20 years from the mid-1960s to the mid-1980s, Japan devoted, on average, nearly one fourth of its GDP to capital investment; the U.S. share averaged less than 14 percent. As a result, the amount of real capital per worker increased nearly 8 percent per year in Japan and so did labor's productivity. In the United States, real capital per worker grew about 3 percent per year, and our productivity by less than that.

We are lagging by a narrower margin in research and development, but the effects may be as serious. New technology enhances the value of additional equipment brought into the production process. In 1988, the United States allocated less than 2 percent of its total output to nonmilitary research and development, while Germany devoted about 2.6 percent, and Japan, 2.8 percent. Corporate America's obsession with the bottom line and the next quarter's earnings are seriously hindering its long-term prospects as an international competitor.

Foreign residents and companies also are raising their relative share of patents awarded in the United States. From 25 percent in 1973, their portion nearly doubled to 48 percent in 1988. In 1978, the top three corporations in numbers of patents awarded were General Electric, Westinghouse, and IBM. In 1988, the first three were Hitachi, Toshiba, and Canon. GE was fourth, and IBM was eighth. Japanese companies held five of the first ten places, and German companies two.

These kinds of activities go to the very heart of competitiveness. Those who would tell you that our poor trade performance is the result of unfair foreign practices or our own budget deficits are barking up the wrong trees. Those trees will bear no fruit (to mix a couple of perfectly innocuous metaphors).

Raising capital investment *will* make us more competitive. It will raise our productivity, our physical capacity, and our standards of living. It is our economy's fountain of youth. And our policymakers keep turning off the spigot. Increasing taxes to cut the budget deficit will not do it. That isn't even an effective way of cutting the deficit.

The Reagan administration did begin to move this economy in the right direction. It was a strong beginning, but toward the end there was some backsliding. The Tax Reform Act of 1986 eliminated important investment incentives and watered down the tax credits for research and development. These were serious errors. The Tax Reform Act needs to be reformed promptly. Soon we will be number three.

Chapter Two

WHY REAGANOMICS WORKED

Myth: Reaganomics was a failure.
Fact: It worked! It produced the longest
peacetime expansion on record.

Ronald Reagan came into office with a few simple economic principles and even simpler economic goals. His presidency achieved great success in the economics area; and if you don't believe it, ask George Bush or Michael Dukakis. Reaganomics was successful because Reagan remained true to his principles—or about as true as it is possible to be in Washington. Basically, with a little oversimplification, his goal was to get the economy growing again; his economic program amounted to "getting the government off your backs and out of your pocketbooks." That may not be as eloquent as New Deal, Fair Deal, New Frontier, or Great Society; but it is less demagogic, a *genuine* deal, and it was right for the times. The proof was America's outstanding economic performance.

Considering the power of the entrenched, vested interests, it is perhaps amazing that the Reagan administration accomplished as much as it did. What vested interests? Not just the old industrial-military complex, but the broader Washington complex, including elected officials, the bureaucracies, lobbyists, advisors, and special interest groups. It's hard to tell where it ends.

The business of Washington is government, and no business—least of all government—seeks to shrink itself. You know what the "bottom line" is for your business or your employer's business. It's earnings, or you're *out* of business. The corresponding bottom line for elected officials is getting reelected. In one sense, government officials—appointed, elected, or entrenched—have it easier than people in private industry, because government does not face a competitive marketplace in its daily operations. So you read about the Defense Department ordering $500 ($1,000?) hammers, toilet seats, or coffee pots; yet those procurement offices are still in business.

To be sure, there is strong competition for elective office. But that is a competition to become eligible to play the game of the three P's—power, privilege, patronage. And that is a popular game indeed. Despite Congress's failure in 1988 to maneuver into effect its own large pay raise, competition for elective office did not diminish. Salaries never have been a disincentive to running for elective office. As economists might say, in terms of supply and demand, salaries are high enough and perhaps too high. Nonetheless, Congressmen did finally get their big pay hike in 1989. It will have little effect on the number or quality of people who run for office.

In 1980, the economy was in trouble. In fact, it was nothing short of a mess. Do you remember the term *stagflation?* It was a combination of *stagnation*—growth had all but disappeared after 1978—and *high inflation*—which was why growth had disappeared. The University of Michigan Index of Consumer Sentiment reached an all-time low in 1980, foreshadowing the election outcome. The country and its people were hurting, and the economy needed bold, new measures. They were not forthcoming from the existing administration, so the country turned to a new one.

The new programs, actually first proposed by candidate Reagan during the primary campaigns, had been denounced as "voodoo economics" by candidate Bush. Of course, not all of the goals were reached; but a good part of the most important ones were—economic growth, jobs, rising incomes and standards of living, and declining poverty rates. But we are getting ahead of ourselves. Nor is it my intention to reheat the political leftovers of the time.

The story really begins in late 1973, an economic watershed for the U.S. economy. I refer to the first oil embargo and price hike by OPEC. But it was not just the price hike; it was also our own haphazard, ineffective distribution of short supplies. To the injury of sharply higher prices was added the insult of many hours, sometimes predawn, in seemingly endless gasoline lines—when you could find gasoline at all.

People began to conserve oil and switched to other energy sources which then rose in price also—although less than oil prices did. Price controls were applied to domestic oil production. But imports accounted for over one third of total supplies, and the effect was devastating. Energy prices rose 17 percent during 1973 and another 22 percent in 1974, boosting the overall consumer price index or CPI by 9 percent in 1973 and 12 percent in 1974—up from a 3.4 percent rise during 1972. The economy went into recession in late 1973 and did not begin to recover until March 1975.

But it could not regain its earlier vitality. Inflation slowed to 5 percent in 1976 because of the recession and began to move up quickly again. It was already back to 9 percent in 1978 before the second oil embargo of 1979 to 1980. The CPI rose more than 13 percent in 1979 and about 12.5 percent in 1980. Meanwhile, interest rates, following inflation, climbed to new peaks. The economy fell into recession in 1980 and again in mid-1981.[1] To get the economy moving, the new president asked for a 30 percent personal tax cut to take effect immediately. But Congress legislated a reduction totaling 25 percent spread over three years. The first installment, which was only 5 percent, was not implemented until October 1981.

From 1973 to 1982, U.S. real gross domestic product (GDP) per capita grew a total of 4.7 percent, or 0.5 percent per year—that is, it barely grew at all. Our economy had grown 2.6 percent per year on average from 1960 to 1973. Growth also slowed in other industrial economies. For example, in Germany growth slipped from 3.5 percent per year to 1.7 percent per year; in Japan growth slowed from 8.5 percent to 2.6 percent—what ours had been for 20 years before the first

---

[1]The Carter administration forbade its officials to use the word *recession*. One member referred to it as a *banana*. Nonetheless, we were not then and are not now becoming a "banana republic."

oil embargo. At least their economies continued to grow, while ours stalled.

The jump in oil prices was not just an exercise in statistical inflation. On the contrary, inflation was the mechanism through which American citizens were required to transfer enormous amounts of income and wealth to OPEC and other oil producers. From 1965 to 1972, oil prices averaged $2 to $3 per barrel. By 1975, the price was close to $12 per barrel; and in 1981, it averaged almost $35 per barrel. Our annual bill for imported oil rose accordingly. From $4.3 billion in 1972, it jumped to $24 billion in 1974 and continued upward to a peak of $78 billion in 1980. The price finally leveled off in 1981.

Prior to 1973, oil consumption (in barrels) in the United States grew at about 4 percent per year, slightly faster than the economy. If oil prices had risen at the same rate as domestic inflation—say, 3 percent per year—that upward trend in consumption might have continued, not indefinitely, but perhaps up to the present time. But after 1973 domestic production leveled off, in spite of higher price levels. This meant that all of the increased consumption was supplied by imports.

If demand continued to grow by 4 percent per year, imports would have had to increase about 11 percent per year to meet that demand. That is because imports constituted less than 40 percent of the total oil supply. Thus, the dollar value of our oil imports, in a free market environment, might have grown about 3 percent in price plus 11 percent in volume, or a total of 14 percent per year—a rather fast growth rate for any commodity for any extended period of time.

Our actual oil bill went up much faster than that. In fact, the total bill for the 16 years from 1973 to 1988 inclusive, exceeded the aforementioned estimated bill (at a generous 14 percent rate of increase) by the enormous amount of $460 billion. That is the *additional* cost imposed by the OPEC cartel. Nearly half of the excess was incurred during the four years 1979 through 1982. Obviously, this dwarfs all of our foreign aid programs combined. It was an enormous tax imposed on our economy and on the American people—where the burden always falls ultimately. No nation has ever paid that amount of reparations—not even after losing a major war. In fact, it far exceeds our entire cost of World War II.

During the 20 years 1953 to 1973, real disposable personal income (RDPI) per capita grew 3.2 percent per year on average. Remember, that is income per person after taxes and after inflation. From 1973 to 1982, because of oil-induced anemic growth in business activity and because of high inflation, we eked out a meager 0.8 percent gain per year. The improvement we might have had in our standards of living during those nine years was turned over to the oil producers.

After 1982, our economy resumed its growth. From 1982 to 1988, RDPI per capita rose about 2.5 percent per year. That was a slightly slower pace than in the pre-1973 period, in part because inflation remained somewhat higher than it was during the pre-1973 period.

To break the siege of stagflation, the Reagan administration proposed new attacks on four fronts: tax cuts to provide incentives for greater economic activity (get the government out of your pocketbooks); government spending cuts to transfer resources to the private economy and, along with faster growth, to help shrink the budget deficit; removal of unnecessary federal regulations to cut business costs and make the economy more competitive (get the government off your backs); and moderate monetary expansion to bring down inflation. The president referred to this package as "America's New Beginning: A Program for Economic Recovery." The program *did* that. It produced not only economic recovery, but the longest continuous peacetime expansion on record.

The hard part was getting the program started. In practice, the four fronts were not coordinated as planned. Furthermore, the economy was even caught in a cross-fire of policies for a brief period.

The Congress did not effect the tax cuts immediately as the president had requested. Instead, they implemented the reductions mainly in 1982 and 1983. The hoped-for quick stimulus to growth was not there; that relief column arrived late.

On a second front, relief in the form of spending cuts never arrived, lost in partisan political dissension. Spending continued to grow rapidly, and the budget deficit threatened to go into orbit. As a result, parts of the tax cuts were rescinded by the Tax Equity and Fiscal Responsibility Act of 1982 (TEFRA for short), mainly by scaling back investment incentives. Deregulation, a third front, assigned to the vice president's office, has remained a minor factor—mainly a diversionary tactic. But monetary policy, the fourth front, did show up promptly and in full force. "Moderation," or restraint, brought down inflation, but it brought down the economy along with it. The economy is not a laboratory. We can try to aim monetary policy at inflation. But in the real world, restricting the supply of money and credit simply raises interest rates—and that usually has adverse effects on both inflation and business activity. The economy indeed was in a cross-fire. Instead of a resurgence in early- to mid-1981, the economy sank into recession again. This lasted until late 1982.

Monetary restraint and the absence of economic recovery began to cause dissent within the administration by the spring of 1982. Well, maybe I was the lone public dissenter. As Chief Economist for the Department of Commerce, I was called frequently by members of the press to comment on the department's data releases. In late spring, Don Regan, then Secretary of the Treasury, accompanied the president to the annual economic summit, this time in Versailles. Regan proceeded to announce to the press and inform the president (probably in that order) that the economy was about to come roaring back. And the president made a similar statement. Unfortunately, our statistics showed that the economy was beginning to weaken again. In response to questions from reporters, I pointed out that the economy was in fact sinking rather than recovering, and that the weakness was the result of tight monetary policy. Interest rates were too high: For example, the prime rate and the rate on home mortgages were still around 16 percent, even though inflation had fallen to less than four percent. Regan's, the president's, and my comments appeared together in the European press.

Not surprisingly, Regan almost immediately contacted Malcolm "Mac" Baldrige, the Secretary of Commerce, to complain about my statements. After all, Regan was the

White House anointed—or maybe just self-appointed—administration "spokesman." The distinction between economic policy issues and statistical reports was too fine to interfere with his exercise of privilege and power. Later on, after he switched jobs with Jim Baker (the one with one k), Regan reportedly referred to himself as the "deputy president." Of course, he was not the only presidential appointee who had a large appetite for power.

I was summoned to Baldrige's office first thing the next morning. And by *first thing,* I mean well before 8 A.M. I crossed half of his cavernous office (a huge office was not unusual for a cabinet member) to his desk; I stood next to his hand-tooled saddle and lariat which, fortunately, he did not unroll at that particular time. He was a genuine cowboy, in case you did not know, and a member of the Cowboy Hall of Fame. I think he was, justifiably, prouder of that membership than of his appointment to the cabinet. In fact, he had left standing instructions that he could be interrupted at any time by only two types of phone calls: the president and any cowboy. As Mac explained it, a cowboy will call only if he actually has something to say.

Mac simply asked me for the facts. And to his great credit, he reviewed them quickly and said, in his inimitable style, "Hell," (not exactly, but close enough—he was a colorful guy), "you're right." And that was the end of the matter. As I was walking toward the door, he called out, "Bob, do me one favor. Try to be aware of when the president is at a summit meeting, and try not to say anything that week."

One of my treasured mementos of government service is a picture of Mac and the president on horseback, on which Mac wrote, "To Bob, a friend and economist who's almost always right." He told me that he added the word *almost* because he was afraid that no one would believe it otherwise. I assured him that it was generous including *almost.*

Throughout my eight-year tour of duty, neither Mac Baldrige nor his able successor Bill Verity ever asked me to do anything other than "tell it like it is." (Mac died tragically in a riding accident in 1987.) But the anecdote does suggest the perilous quality of life in Washington. Had I joined Treasury and Regan, instead of Commerce and Baldrige, my public service would have been much shorter, probably by about seven years.

By late 1982, the Federal Reserve had loosened its monetary noose, permitting the new tax programs to begin to breathe life into the economy. The prime rate was down to about 11 percent, and mortgage rates to less than 13 percent. Still not "cheap money" but, considering their 1981 respective peaks of 21 percent and 18 percent, apparently livable.

During the Reagan years, Congress enacted a number of fiscal packages. The most important were the Economic Recovery Tax Act of 1981 (ERTA—Washington lives by acronyms) and the Tax Reform Act of 1986 (TRA—no *la la*— although that might have been appropriate). ERTA provided across-the-board cuts in individual rates, and thereby stimulated stronger consumer spending. Perhaps more importantly, the act strengthened investment incentives through provisions for accelerated depreciation of equipment and structures. The Investment Tax Credit was already in place.

These incentives were both necessary and overdue. From the mid-1960s through the 1970s, U.S. real gross domestic investment grew an average of only 2.1 percent per year—one of the worst records among the industrial countries. But when the economy rebounded, capital spending was a front-running sector. Despite a decline during the 1981 to 1982 recession, real investment grew at an average rate of 5.6 percent a year from 1981 through 1986.[2] And this was one of the best records among the industrial countries. It was also a key aspect of the success of Reagan's economic program.

In the Tax Reform Act of 1986, the president achieved a long-term goal of lowering tax rates. The original name, by the way, was Tax Simplification and Reform Act. At least Congress had the grace to drop *Simplification* from the title. In 1976, Jimmy Carter called our patch-work, complicated tax system a disgrace. He was right. Even with fewer brackets today, it is still a disgrace. And the government is beginning to tinker with it again.

---

[2]*Economic Report of the President,* January 1989, p. 90.

But the lower tax rates were achieved at a high cost. Under pressure of ongoing and disappointingly high budget deficits, the administration and Congress agreed that the rate reductions would have to be paid for by increases in other areas, so that the overall package would be "revenue-neutral."

On the personal side, elimination of some shelters and benefits only partly offset the effects of sharply lower rates. Therefore, individual taxes were cut substantially. Corporate tax rates (not total taxes) also were reduced—from 46 percent to 34 percent. But to pay for this reduction, investment incentives were cut drastically. The Investment Tax Credit was eliminated, and accelerated depreciation was scaled back for structures. The net effect was to raise corporate taxes.

Under the Tax Reform Act, the effective tax rate on equipment is expected to rise from 10 percent to nearly 40 percent, primarily because of eliminating the Investment Tax Credit; while the effective rate on nonresidential structures will rise from 34 percent to 43 percent.[3] These tax measures, would you believe, were enacted at the same time that the Congress was arguing that we must find new ways to improve U.S. competitiveness! Such is life in Washington, where the paths of reality and rhetoric cross only occasionally; and unfortunately for the American people, they did not meet in 1986.

Proponents of the Tax Reform Act argue that lower personal rates will encourage more work. I agree. But rising productivity and standards of living depend on improving technology and a growing capital base. Mankind could have improved its lot during the stone age by working harder and harder; but without the improving technology and tools, we would still be in the stone age. By eliminating the Investment Tax Credit, we are in effect stifling our economic growth.

The corporate side of the Tax Reform Act was a serious mistake. The next fiscal change should reinstate the Investment Tax Credit. To encourage the Democratic members of Congress, perhaps it should be pointed out that it was first enacted during the Kennedy administration.

---

[3]Ibid., p. 93.

Improving depreciation allowances would also stimulate more investment. Either or both of these measures would be highly effective in promoting real investment growth. But I am afraid that the White House is focusing on the wrong measure—looking at the financial market instead of the real economy. President Bush proposed lowering the capital gains rate in 1989. Unfortunately, for the purpose of promoting real investment, a lower capital gains rate would be far less effective than reinstating the Investment Tax Credit or increasing depreciation allowances.[4]

Meanwhile, back at the (economic) ranch, Table 2–1 contains many of the important measures that describe the economy, its trials, and its rehabilitation. The consumer price index (CPI) and the prime rate are near the center of the table. Their paths and effects on the economy are clear. Following the 1973 to 1975 recession, the recovery carried through 1978, with strong gains in industrial production and real GNP. But inflation and interest rates were already on the rise, and they strangled the economy in the 1979 to 1982 period.

The lack of growth in these years meant, of course, no new jobs. At the same time, the labor force continued to expand, so that the unemployment rate reached 10.7 percent by the end of 1982—its highest level since World War II. The unemployment rate had begun to rise in 1979, nearing 8 percent when the 1981 recession began; that was also the highest postwar rate at the beginning of any recession.

The so-called Misery Index, a simple sum of unemployment and inflation, reached 19.5 at the end of 1980 and then declined as inflation came down after 1980 and unemployment fell after 1982. But as I indicated earlier, economic ebb and flow is not just a matter of statistical description. It is a matter of livelihoods and standards of living. The lack of job gains translated into no gain in real disposable personal income in the aggregate and some slippage on a per capita

---

[4]Results obtained from the Bureau of Economic Analysis econometric model.

TABLE 2–1
Measures of Economic Performance

	1978	1979	1980	1981	1982	1983	1984	1985	1986	1987	1988	1989
Misery index[a]	14.9	19.2	19.5	17.3	14.6	12.0	11.2	10.7	7.8	10.1	9.7	9.9
Consumer sentiment[b]	66.1	61.0	64.5	64.3	71.9	94.2	92.9	93.9	89.1	86.8	91.9	90.5
Percent Change from Year End to Year End												
Industrial production	8.5	0.2	0.0	-3.2	-6.4	14.9	6.2	2.2	1.1	5.4	4.9	1.7
Real GNP	6.3	0.6	-0.1	0.6	-1.9	6.5	5.1	3.6	1.9	5.4	3.4	2.4
Manufacturing productivity	2.3	-1.3	1.5	1.0	3.9	5.4	5.4	4.5	3.3	3.8	2.9	2.6
Real disposable personal income	4.7	0.5	1.7	-0.4	1.9	5.1	4.3	2.7	3.3	3.0	4.0	3.7
CPI	9.0	13.3	12.4	8.9	3.9	3.8	4.0	3.8	1.1	4.4	4.4	4.6
Exchange rate[c]	7.1	1.4	1.0	9.0	11.0	6.0	9.7	-10.3	-11.7	-15.8	2.4	4.1
Prime rate (%)[d]	11.6	15.3	20.35	15.75	11.50	11.00	11.06	9.50	7.50	8.75	10.50	10.00
End of Year Level												
Civilian employment (millions)	97.6	99.9	99.6	99.6	99.0	103.0	106.2	108.1	110.7	113.7	116.0	117.9
Unemployment rate (%) including armed forces	5.9	5.9	7.1	8.4	10.7	8.2	7.2	6.9	6.7	5.7	5.3	5.3
Labor force participation rate	63.9	64.2	63.9	64.0	64.5	64.5	65.0	65.3	65.6	66.1	66.4	66.8
Employment/ population ratio (%)	60.2	60.5	59.4	58.6	57.6	59.2	60.3	60.8	61.3	62.3	62.9	63.3
Merchandise Trade Deficit ($Bil, annual rate, NIPA basis)												
Nominal $	25.6	35.3	20.9	30.2	43.6	82.7	114.7	143.7	148.3[e]	158.0	127.8	112.7
1982 $	70.9	47.8	-10.9[f]	26.8	43.6	97.2	132.3	155.9	182.2[e]	148.7	124.8	109.4
Federal Budget Deficit, fiscal years, % of GNP	2.7	1.6	2.8	2.6	4.1	6.3	5.0	5.4	5.3	3.4	3.2	2.9

[a] Inflation during the year plus year-end unemployment rate.
[b] End of year level, index 1Q 1966 = 100.
[c] U.S. trade-weighted value of the dollar, 15 currencies, Morgan Guaranty Bank.
[d] End-of-year level.
[e] 3Q rather than 4Q.
[f] Merchandise trade surplus.

33

basis. This explains why the University of Michigan Index of Consumer Sentiment fell to an all-time low level in early 1980.

The expansion that began in late 1982 has been the longest on record during peacetime, surely an outstanding accomplishment. In the six years through the end of 1988, industrial production rose almost 40 percent, an average of 5.75 percent per year; and real GNP grew a total of almost 28 percent, an average of 4.25 percent per year. Along with growth in output, 17 million new jobs were added through the end of 1988. Workers to fill those jobs came from two sources: a large pool of unemployed people available at the beginning of the expansion and new entrants or reentrants into the labor force during the expansion.

By the end of 1988, the unemployment rate was down to 5.3 percent, its lowest level in over 14 years. Table 2–1 also shows a measure of the number of workers entering the labor force—the labor force participation rate. At the end of 1980, 63.9 percent of the population of working age were in the labor force; by the end of 1988, encouraged by job opportunities and by lower tax rates, 66.4 percent of the working-age population were "participating." This was an all-time high.

As a result of strong job growth and the high participation rate, 62.9 percent of the population were *employed* at the end of 1988. (This percentage is lower than the participation rate above, because not everyone participating is working). This also constituted an all-time high, up from 57.6 percent at the end of 1982. To illustrate just how strong this job performance was, consider the following: Given the actual level of employment, had the labor force participation rate remained at 1980's 63.9 percent, the unemployment rate at the end of 1988 would have been down to almost 2 percent!

But we never would have made it. Long before reaching that low an unemployment rate, inflation would have boiled up, and—one way or another—the business expansion would have slowed or ended. We would have had neither 17 million additional jobs nor the gains in total real incomes.

Thus, one way of achieving economic growth is through an expanding labor force. That means aggregate growth, but not necessarily growth in real output per capita or real income per capita. In order to maintain real gains per capita, we must have growth in productivity. Growth in productivity brings technical advancement and capital investment into the economic picture once more.

It is interesting to find that this trade-off between unemployment and inflation is not universal. Switzerland, for example, currently has about 1 percent unemployment (that is not a misprint—1 percent!) and about 4 percent inflation. It is widely accepted that their inflation is limited by importing foreign workers. However, I believe that the effect of this labor influx on their inflation is exaggerated. Inflation remains moderate there because of a national antipathy toward it, and because of more responsible attitudes of both business and labor. They accept the reality that high inflation is detrimental to the economy as well as the individual. In practice, their system of cooperation has produced one of the highest living standards in the world.

In the United States and in the United Kingdom to an even greater extent, the system is confrontational. The emphasis is on maximizing pay increases and/or price increases and unfortunately not on productivity. This system cannot win in the long run. But we digress—back to the short run.

The Index of Consumer Sentiment jumped to about 90 in 1983 and stayed near that level through the entire period. Twice again the index correctly predicted the election outcomes. This time favorably for the party in office in 1984 and 1988. While his own coattails proved too short to carry Republican legislators into office in 1988, Mr. Bush found it easy sailing on Mr. Reagan's coattails.

I am not going to claim discovery of an infallible predictor of election results, for two good reasons. First, I have been around long enough to know that as soon as one devises a new "infallible" leading indicator, whether it pertains to the stock market, the economy or to the political arena, it immediately becomes fallible. Second, the index may work when it is at very high or very low levels, in which case you do not need it; but it will probably prove unreliable at middle levels—say, 75 to 85, where it will be most of the time.

A political argument arose during this period regarding the nation's least affluent groups. The debate centered on whether the nation's poor and minorities benefited from the business expansion. Undoubtedly, there were some "pockets of resistance," but, generally, the benefits were widespread. I believe it was Jack Kennedy who once said that a rising tide lifts all boats. From 1982 to 1988, not too many boats ran aground.

Each summer or fall, the Commerce Department's Census Bureau reports data on the nation's average family income and on the number of families "in poverty." The poverty rates are based on minimum income estimates originally drawn up in 1964 by the Social Security Administration, and updated by federal interagency committees.[5] The census data are reported in two ways—money income alone and money income plus noncash benefits such as Medicaid, food stamps, and public housing.

For 1988, the government's cash-income poverty threshold was $12,092 for a family of four and ranged from $6,024 for a single individual to $24,133 for a household of nine persons or more. Appropriately, the poverty threshold is adjusted each year for changes in consumer prices. Rising prices require at least commensurate gains in income "to keep the wolf from the door."

It is not surprising that these data follow the same general patterns as the overall economy. Median family income measured in constant 1988 prices reached a peak in 1973 at $32,109 and, with the "help" of slow growth and fast inflation, bottomed at $28,727 in 1982.

Then with resumed economic growth, more jobs, and slower inflation, median family income—still measured in 1988 prices—finally reached a new peak of $32,251 in 1987 and leveled off in 1988. The 1987 and 1988 family incomes were barely above their 1973 level. That translates into virtually no gain in 15 years. Were it not for the business

---

[5]*Money Income and Poverty Status in the United States: 1987,* U.S. Department of Commerce, Bureau of the Census, Appendix A.

expansion after 1982, family incomes would still be well below 1973 levels. From 1982 to 1988, median family income, in real purchasing power, gained nearly 12 percent.

Similarly, the estimated poverty rate rose from 11.1 percent in 1973 to 12.3 percent in 1975. It eased to 11.4 percent in 1978 and then rose steadily to about 15 percent in 1982 to 1983 before declining again to 13.1 percent in 1988. If noncash benefits such as food, shelter, and Medicaid, measured at market values, were included in the measure of family incomes, the poverty rate would have been several percentage points lower. However, the general trend would have been the same.

While government policies can promote a stronger economy and so lift most—if not all—boats, the same census reports show that private, individual efforts can also help dramatically. Two individual characteristics that were important were education and family status. The median income for households whose "head" or chief provider had fewer than 4 years of high school education was $14,142; while households whose chief provider completed four years of college had a median income of $45,490. Similarly, families headed by married couples had a median income of $36,436 regardless of education; median income for families headed by a single female householder amounted to only $16,051.

The economic performance after 1982 was clearly outstanding, especially when compared with the previous decade. In the fall of 1987, I had the honor to be invited to testify at a hearing of the Joint Economic Committee of the Congress of the United States. Senator Paul Sarbanes of Maryland chaired the hearing. After I had described the economic developments of the 1980s, either he or Congressman Stephen Solarz of New York, or both, quickly retorted: "Well, Dr. Ortner, you've given us a Pollyanna view of the economy," or words very close to those. "What about the budget deficits and all that public debt that we've piled up?" they asked. Obviously, they believe that the budget deficits will wipe out the economic gains since 1982. Don't worry. They won't.

Without question, the federal budget deficit has been one of the most talked about issues and the most exaggerated economic problem of the late 1980s. This has been essentially a specious political argument. It is something for the "out" party to complain about in election campaigns. But it did not work in 1988; the public had better sense and was not that gullible.

Not long after he left Washington, President Reagan's first Director of the Office of Management and Budget (OMB), David Stockman, wrote a book in which he pronounced Reaganomics a failure.[6] Obviously, he was not talking about the economy—that part of Reaganomics was a rousing success—but about the budget deficits.

If there was a failure, it was in slowing down government spending—and that was Stockman's responsibility as head of OMB. After all, it was understood in Washington that Reagan hired him because he had a reputation of knowing his way around the corridors of Congress. Or as Henny Youngman might have put it, better he should have known his way around the members of Congress. Somehow, Stockman's comments remind me of Alexander Pope's line, "The proper study of mankind is man." "Well . . . ," as Reagan used to say, the proper study of Reaganomics is economics—the economy. The budget deficit is a small part of the total economic picture, and it is not a serious problem anyway.

Now consider this statement: "By now [written in 1988] it is clear that Reagan's fiscal policy has achieved *none* [emphasis added] of its advertised economic objectives." What can this possibly mean? I spent nearly eight years in the Commerce Department and could not avoid seeing the administration's great delight when the stagflation was broken and further elation at the strong growth in output, jobs, incomes, and living standards. Judging from the University of Michigan Survey of Consumer Sentiment, the public was equally, or probably more, delighted.

Who could have written that quoted sentence? Benjamin Friedman, a Harvard Professor and, I am told, economic

---

[6]David A. Stockman, *The Triumph of Politics* (New York: Harper and Row, 1986).

advisor to Michael Dukakis in 1988.[7] The quote may also remind you of one of Reagan's favorite jokes: It takes a Ph.D in economics to be able to avoid understanding the obvious.

Friedman goes on: "The share of the nation's income devoted to investment in business plant and equipment—or for that matter to investment of any kind—is not up but down compared to prior experience."[8] Now, "investment in business plant and equipment" is pretty specific. In our national income accounts (GNP accounts), one component is business fixed investment in equipment and structures. During the 1950s, this component averaged about 9.9 percent of real GNP; during the 1960s, 10.3 percent of real GNP; in the 1970s, 11.1 percent; in 1980 through 1988, 11.7 percent; in 1985 and 1988, the share was over 12 percent. Clearly, the trend has been gradually up, not down. Yet, I will agree with part of Dr. Friedman's complaint. It isn't good enough. Our competitors do better and so can we. We should attempt to raise our investment share of GNP substantially.

Lamenting the federal budget deficits of the 1980s, Friedman concludes in Chapter 1 of *Day of Reckoning* that "America has thrown itself a party and billed the tab to the future."[9] Just what party has been thrown is ambiguous and the notion of billing the tab to the future is political rhetoric. As I will show in the next chapter, the assertion that the budget deficits of the 1980s represent a burden for our children and grandchildren has no foundation in economic theory or in historical fact.

Just before I left the Commerce Department in March 1989, a colleague asked me: "Bob, I know you argue that these budget deficits are not very important. But tell me the truth. What were you saying in the early 1960s about the Kennedy-Johnson tax cuts and deficits?" "That's easy," I answered, "I'm consistent. I said the same thing. I was a Democrat then."

---

[7]Benjamin M. Friedman, *Day of Reckoning* (New York: Random House, 1988), p. 86.
[8]Ibid.
[9]Ibid., p. 4.

In early 1981, I wrote that not all of the president's goals would be realized (very different from "none"). Because of tight monetary policy in 1981, initial economic growth, budgetary receipts, and budget deficits would be disappointing.[10] Nonetheless, my assessment then of the new program was that we should go for it. I still feel the same way.

Average growth through the next few years will be slower than it was from 1982 through 1988. However, the slowing is not because of the budget or trade deficits, as it is widely claimed, but because the American economy at the end of 1988 was already fully utilizing its real resources of labor and industrial plant. From here on, economic growth will depend more on growth in productivity. In 1989, one effect of full employment was already evident—some signs of a pickup in inflation. On the economic front, therefore, Mr. Bush faces a tougher challenge than Mr. Reagan did at the start of his administration.

---

[10]Robert Ortner, "America's New Beginning: A Program for Economic Recovery," article distributed by The Bank of New York, February 26, 1981.

Chapter Three

WE OWE IT TO OURSELVES

Myth: The federal debt will strangle our
economy and is a terrible burden
that we're passing on to our
children.

Fact: The debt is moderate in relation
to our economy; it will not be paid
off; and for the most part we owe
it to ourselves.

Now, don't get me wrong. I
don't like budget deficits. I'm not advocating them for their
own sake. Just like everyone else, I'd like a balanced budget.
But here we are, with a $150 billion or so deficit and more
than $2 trillion in federal debt held by the public. How serious
is the deficit or the debt? How did we get there? What should
we do about it?

Journalists, politicians, and Nobel Prize winners alike,
have proclaimed the federal budget deficits and debt to be
America's most serious economic problems. And they assert
that eliminating the deficit—by spending cuts, by tax
increases, or preferably by both—must be our highest
priority. But the facts show that these deficits and debt are
a greatly exaggerated problem, if they are a problem at all.
Those who are calling for higher taxes want the additional
revenue to finance existing or new spending programs; or
they philosophically prefer larger to smaller governments;
or perhaps they simply do not understand the issue.

My advice to you, the public, is to keep your money at home—you will get a much better return if you invest your funds in your own business or in the financial markets. With regard to these deficits, it's *earlier* than you think—or earlier than they would have you believe.

When Ronald Reagan took office, federal outlays amounted to nearly 23 percent of GNP. Spending was rising rapidly. The economy was not rising at all. It had just emerged from one recession and was about to enter another. The Reagan administration sought to slow spending and speed up economic growth partly through the fiscal stimulation of cutting taxes. One goal was to bring spending and receipts to less than 20 percent of GNP. This was where they were during the 1950s and 1960s. These patterns are shown in Chart 3–1.

The tax cuts did the job for receipts, but spending was another matter. The 1980 to 1982 recessions meant no growth in GNP. Continued increases in outlays lifted spending to about 24 percent of GNP in the years 1983 to 1985. As a

CHART 3–1
Federal Outlays and Receipts (As Percent of GNP)

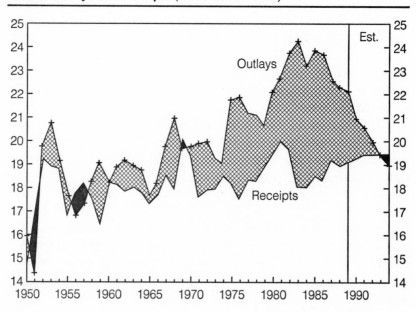

result, the federal budget deficit ballooned to over $200 billion in 1985 and 1986.

The administration was probably naive in thinking that the Congress could be disciplined or shamed by the deficits into cutting, or even holding the line on, spending. The members of Congress have their own agenda, if not their own goals. Cutting spending is okay if it is the "other guy's." After all, spending means dollars for the folks back home—a "free lunch," as it were. In that sense, spending is as good as, and sometimes better than, campaign funds.

At one point, I was personally affected by one spending scheme. President Reagan nominated me to be Under Secretary of the Department of Commerce in March 1986. My hearing before the Senate Commerce Committee was scheduled promptly, and after my testimony, the committee voted unanimously in favor of my confirmation. The process could have been completed quickly—within a week or two—with a routine vote by the full Senate. But I was informed by Commerce's congressional liaison officer that my nomination was "on hold" and the Senate would not vote on it for some indefinite period.

"How come?" I asked. Well, it seemed that one senator, Bob Kasten, Republican of Wisconsin, had applied to the Economic Development Administration for a grant to improve a marina at Racine. A marina, mind you, at taxpayer expense. The Commerce Department, to its credit, turned him down. "But," I protested, "that's a different part of the department and has nothing to do with me." "Sure," the liaison officer said, "but it doesn't matter. Kasten's angry at the department, and you, Ortner, are the hostage," or words very close to those.

After several months of discussion (negotiation?) between the department and the senator, he was finally given some other, more appropriate, grant—and certainly not at my request. I was confirmed by the full Senate in July, nearly four months after my nomination.

This process, I later learned, occurs with great regularity in Washington. It is not a rare occurrence. But the Congress does not have to perform this sort of charade to spend money. They can appropriate and mandate funds in the normal budget process. The trouble is that cutting or limiting spending is thankless, generally resulting in a bias toward growing outlays.

A number of years ago, then Representative Paul Simon, Democrat of Illinois, wrote to his constituents: "We must bring spending and revenue into line. You can be part of the solution. When you write to your representatives asking for an additional service, add a second paragraph noting that you are willing to pay the taxes for it. If you are unwilling to write the second paragraph, don't write the first one." Each appropriations committee should be required to reread this statement before each vote. It might make it easier to "just say no." After all, our government should provide occasional leadership, or maybe backbone, along with the "pork." And *leadership* is not synonymous with *spending*.

Congressional calls for tax increases are not intended solely for deficit reduction. They are also for spending maintenance. President Reagan once quipped that the Congress reminded him of an old definition of a baby—a delightful little critter with an insatiable appetite at one end and no sense of responsibility at the other.

Outside the beltway and outside the bond market, the public does not seem persuaded by the pleas and arguments for higher taxes. But I think they are persuaded that much waste remains in government. Both Presidential candidates in 1988 understood this: Michael Dukakis softened his call for a tax increase to a whisper and George Bush denounced it. While Mr. Dukakis never really changed his position, Mr. Bush had come half circle, at least publicly, from "voodoo economics" in 1980 to "read my lips" in 1988. Well . . . , as Reagan used to say, I suppose that's being responsive to the will of the electorate; and in a practical sense, if you can't beat them, why not join them?

But we do have ongoing budget deficits. Do they mean that there is a serious problem lurking around the corner? Are we heading for a fall? A *Wall Street Journal* article in January 1989 headlined "The Budget Albatross" began, "The deficit hangs like an albatross around his [President Bush's] neck, hindering his movements in every direction."[1] A more severe critic asks, "What can you say to a man on a binge who asks why it matters?" So Professor Benjamin Friedman began his book and, by analogy, concluded that borrowing is just as bad for the U.S. government.[2] Of course, I would say to the man in the analogy that he is a damn fool.

Analogies are often inaccurate and misleading—perhaps even dangerous. Suppose the man borrowed the money from his wife, spent part, but invested enough so that the family's total assets increased in value. Is the family worse off or better off than before? The family surely is more analogous to the country than is the man.

Paul Samuelson, the first American Nobel Prize winner in economics and author of the country's most successful economics textbook, lists several logical fallacies that students should recognize. Samuelson refers to one of them as "The fallacy of composition," which states that what is true of a part is therefore alleged or believed to be true of the whole.[3] Mr. Friedman's leap from his man to the federal deficit is an excellent example of this fallacy.

Mr. Friedman goes on: "We have enjoyed what appears to be a higher . . . standard of living by selling our and our children's economic birthright."[4] Many others have also lamented the burden of debt we have allegedly hung on our economy and bequeathed to our children. But have we really burdened either our economy or our children? Or sold their birthright?

In 1989, total federal debt amounted to a little less than $3 trillion. But the federal government itself held about $675.0 billion, with about $2.2 trillion held by the public. With the 1989 population estimated at close to 245 million,

---

[1]"A *WSJ* Report, The Inauguration," *The Wall Street Journal,* Friday, January 20, 1989, p. R16.

[2]Benjamin M. Friedman, *Day of Reckoning* (New York: Random House, 1988), p. 1.

[3]Paul Samuelson and William D. Nordhaus, *Economics* 13th ed. (New York: McGraw-Hill, 1989), p. 8.

[4]Friedman, *Day of Reckoning,* p. 5.

the $2.2 trillion debt outstanding "amounts to roughly $9,000 for every man, woman, and child," as the doomsayers warn you. And this is the alleged burden we are supposedly passing on to our children for them to repay. A terrible burden indeed!

But will they ever have to repay it? And what does repaying it mean anyway? Just as budget deficits add to the debt, *repayment* simply means running budget surpluses. For example, surpluses of $220 billion a year for only 10 years (I'm kidding) would do it; and, of course, so would $22 billion a year for 100 years. But virtually no one is advocating this course.

The arguments concern only how to bring the budget into balance and how quickly we should try to do that. There are even some very respectable and respected economists who argue that *in real terms*—that is, after adjusting for inflation—today's deficits are small and should not be reduced at all.

But just suppose our policymakers did embark on a program of paying off the national debt. What would happen mechanically? Well, the cash generated by budget surpluses would be paid out to retire the $2.2 trillion of treasury securities outstanding. But paid out to whom? To us, of course, the public—individuals, foundations, business firms, pension funds, financial institutions—all of us who *own* these treasury securities. The treasury securities outstanding are our assets, as well as federal obligations. And as assets, they still amount to $9,000 for every man, woman, and child. Why, we are rich!

But, you say, you don't own any, and if you were required to pay taxes to run a budget surplus to retire the debt, you would be a loser. But rest easy, you don't have to worry. If you hold no government obligations, and have no bank accounts, company pensions, IRA or Keogh plans, or life insurance policies (these institutions would have invested your funds at least partly in treasury securities), and have few other assets and little income, you would not be required to pay the taxes to retire the debt. In legislating tax increases, your representatives would invoke a favorite slogan like *tax equity* or *tax fairness*. And who can disagree with fairness?

In practice, these tax slogans mean "hitting" corporations and upper income individuals. But those are the groups I hope we can convince—with the help of tax incentives—to raise their rate of investment in new plant and equipment and thereby raise the nation's productivity and all of our incomes. Hitting them with new taxes surely would not induce them to invest more.

And what would happen after the money is paid back to the public in exchange for the government's debt? I bet the public would soon begin to pressure their representatives to create new federal debt so that they would be able to invest their money in "riskless" government securities. So why bother in the first place?

But isn't $2.2 trillion in government debt so large that it may put a burden on our economy or impede its operation? Indeed, the sum is so large it is mind-boggling. Nonetheless, it can be viewed as an individual's debt can be, from the perspective of wealth and the economy's ability to carry it. Suppose Mr. Friedman's man suddenly takes on a $100,000 debt. Does this mean—as Mr. Micawber might say—"misery?" So far, we do not know. This cannot be determined from the debt alone. At one extreme, if the new debt resulted from gambling losses and the man has no assets and little income to cover it, we can say with great confidence that he is in trouble. (Probably in more ways than one.)

Alternatively, suppose the new debt represented a mortgage against the purchase of, say, a $300,000 home and that the man has an annual income of $200,000 or more and no other indebtedness or extraordinary obligations. It would appear that the man, far from Mr. Micawber's state of misery, is in great shape.

Certainly we would not consider advising the man to sell his home in order to pay off his mortgage obligation. That would be nonsense. If his home were appreciating in value and his income growing, most reasonable financial analysts would advise him that he could, if he wished, take on and safely carry still more liabilities. At the other extreme, if the man is into his bookies and cannot pay, my advice to him would be to get out of town—today—and change his identity.

Similar, if not identical, relationships may be used in analyzing the federal debt. Did you know that the federal government owns vast amounts of assets? According to the Bureau of Economic Analysis (BEA), an arm of the U.S. Department of Commerce, at the end of 1988 the federal government held nearly $1.5 trillion worth of equipment and structures, not including normal operating inventories.[5] In addition, the federal government owns vast amounts of land, mineral rights, oil reserves, gold reserves, and financial assets. The Federal Reserve banks, for example, hold well over $200 billion of treasury securities. In all, priced at current market values, these assets are worth more than the federal debt outstanding. Your government, in fact, has a positive net worth.

I suppose that adding up these assets and liabilities may give one a quieting sense of federal fiscal solvency, but it is a purely academic exercise (academic in the sense that Mark Twain would have used the term—irrelevant and useless). The federal government is not for sale, will not be liquidated, and will not be available for a leveraged buyout. Nor are its bonds in any danger of falling into "junk" status. On the contrary, its obligations are universally regarded as the highest standard of quality. And that is because its debt is moderate in relation to its assets and—more importantly—moderate in relation to the economy.

Government debt is also highly regarded because it is backed by two other assets not included in a customary balance sheet tally: the government's almost unlimited ability to tax (short of killing the goose that lays these golden tax eggs) and its almost unlimited ability to borrow (while its debt remains of moderate proportions). For these reasons, no business firm—not even the highest quality "Triple-A" borrower—can raise funds in the free market on terms as favorable as the U.S. treasury can.

Realistically, the government's debt and its annual deficits must be viewed on a going-concern basis. The more interesting and meaningful questions concern relationships between the debt and budget deficits on one side and the

---

[5]Bureau of Economic Analysis, *Survey of Current Business* (Washington, D.C.: U.S. Department of Commerce, August 1989), p. 92, Table 13.

economy on the other. Can the economy carry this amount of debt? Will it be stifled by this debt or by the budget deficits? A little historical perspective should help to answer these questions and help to calm your fears.

Most economists use gross national product (GNP) to represent the economy. GNP is our best single measure of total economic output, and it is from this output that we earn our incomes. We also customarily refer to or imply GNP when we discuss economic growth. As large as the federal debt appears at 1989's $2.2 trillion, the figure has little meaning unless we consider it within the context of our economy—an economy that produced about $5.25 trillion in goods and services in 1989. That means that this "burdensome" debt amounts to about 42 percent of GNP.

While 42 percent is a more comprehensible figure, it still requires some historical perspective for its significance. Chart 3-2 shows this record since the early 1950s along with the same ratio to GNP for nonfinancial private debts. Financial institutions are not included, because they are in the business of borrowing and relending. Their inclusion would exaggerate and distort the totals. And before you become duly concerned about borrowing in the private sector, let's focus on the federal debt.

Clearly, federal debt has grown faster than the economy since 1981. Three basic factors account for this acceleration: failure of the economy to begin to recover until the end of 1982; the tax cuts that were phased in from 1981 to 1983; and continued rapid growth in government spending. The low point in the ratio of debt to GNP was slightly over 24 percent in 1974. But note that in the early 1950s, federal debt was still about two thirds of GNP. I say "still" because toward the end of World War II, federal debt *exceeded* GNP—that is, it was more than 100 percent of GNP. Certainly, the "heavy debt burden" did not destroy the economy then. In fact, many economists and critics of the Reagan administration point out that the country enjoyed faster growth in the 1950s than it did during the recovery years of the 1980s.

If today's U.S. debt, at 42 percent of GNP, raises concerns, it is understandable that the huge federal borrowing of World War II caused great anxiety. Professor Evsey D. Domar, then

CHART 3–2
U.S. Government & Private Debt Outstanding (Relative to GNP)

a member of the Federal Reserve Board's division of research and statistics, wrote:

> On November 30, 1945 the federal debt reached 265 billion dollars, a magnitude without precedent in the history of the country. . . . It is quite understandable that a debt of this magnitude should cause considerable apprehension, and that a policy of repaying at least a part of it should be advocated so often.

But rather than join the crowd in a knee-jerk reaction demanding higher taxes, Domar advocated a gradual solution in a broader economic context:

> The greater is the rate of growth of income, the lower will be the ratio of debt and of interest charges to income. . . . Repayment of the debt is *not* the only available method of reducing

the debt burden. This aim can also be achieved, and in a much safer way, by promoting a more rapid growth of income. That the latter is desirable of itself is evident.[6]

These comments, which proved accurate then, are just as relevant today.

Today's debt at 42 percent of GNP is about average for the postwar period, and it appears to be leveling off. To reduce this ratio, we do not have to run a budget surplus or even eliminate the deficit. All that is required is that the debt grow at a slower percentage rate than the economy does. For example, if the economy were to grow at a 7 percent rate for an extended period of time (say, 3 percent real plus 4 percent inflation), the debt would have to grow slightly slower. Let's say, it grew 6 percent per year. On a base of $2.2 trillion, a 6 percent increase would mean a budget deficit now of $132 billion. And if the deficit remained at $132 billion, the growth rate in total debt outstanding would slow as the debt became larger.

Yes, we can aim to reduce the ratio of debt to GNP and lower successive budget deficits gradually. But we should not forget that our ultimate goal is to improve economic performance. The purpose of conducting fiscal and monetary policies is to promote and enhance, if possible, sustainable economic growth. We should not be manipulating the economy for the sake of fiscal performance.

Some economists believe that our budget deficit is now tolerable and that the economic health of our nation would be undermined if we reduced the deficit. In a series of articles, Professor Robert Eisner, a recent president of the American Economic Association, points out that the significance of the budget deficit is not what it appears on the surface to be. He argues that two kinds of adjustments should be applied to the budget data: One is accounting for investment outlays—not all government spending is for current consumption—and the

---

[6]"Public Debt and National Income," in *Public Finance and Full Employment* (Washington, D.C.: Board of Governors of the Federal Reserve System, December 1945), p. 53.

other is adjusting for inflation in order to obtain estimates of deficits in real terms and thereby assess their impacts on the real economy.[7]

His contention regarding government investment is simple. Business firms do not include in each year's income statements their entire investment outlays. If they purchase machinery and equipment and construct plants or office buildings, only the amounts "used up," or depreciated, in a current year are shown as expense. The investments are placed in the firms' capital budgets and in their balance sheets.

The government does not have a capital budget. All investments are expensed, which Eisner claims overstates current spending and exaggerates the deficits. Certainly, compared with normal, private accounting procedures, this is true. The budget submitted by the Reagan administration in January 1989 estimated total outlays of $1,137 billion for 1989 and a deficit of $162 billion. The budget documents also estimated federal investment outlays of $214 billion, included in total spending.

Establishing a capital budget would not mean, however, that the 1989 budget actually was in surplus. We would have to add depreciation charges for existing capital stock to expenditures. I indicated earlier that at the end of 1988, the federal government owned nearly $1.5 trillion in equipment and structures—$1.434 trillion to be more precise. Of this sum, it held $748 billion in equipment and $687 billion in structures. If the government depreciated the equipment in 5 years and the structures in 30, it would have incurred total depreciation charges of about $173 billion. Thus, subtracting investment outlays of $214 billion and adding depreciation charges of $173 billion would have reduced the projected 1989 budget deficit from $162 billion to $121 billion—a more reasonable portrayal, perhaps, by business accounting standards.

---

[7]Robert Eisner and Paul J. Pieper, "A New View of the Federal Debt and Budget Deficits," *The American Economic Review,* March 1984, pp. 11–28. See also Robert Eisner, *How Real Is The Federal Deficit?* (New York: The Free Press, 1989); and "Op-Ed" articles in the *Washington Post,* February 2, 1984; and *New York Times,* May 4, 1986; and a letter to the editor, *New York Times,* February 19, 1989.

One important reason businesses follow this procedure is to provide an accounting of their profits and losses. This, of course, is not of concern in government operations. Nonetheless, capital budgeting would help to provide a more accurate description of government operations, provide the public with better information regarding the allocation of government funds, and make it easier to trace the accumulations of government debt and assets.

One thing would not change. An important factor regarding government activities is the impact of its borrowing on credit markets. Whether borrowing is for current activity or long-term investment, we would still want to know the government's total borrowing requirements. This figure is more accurately provided by today's form of budgeting than by a current expense budget alone. If we were to adopt the new accounting system, data on the additional financing requirements would still have to be provided.

Professor Eisner also recommends adjusting the budget deficit for inflation to get a "real" picture of it. After all, we do that for most economic data—GNP, incomes, retail sales, etc.—to be able to understand their true significance. As the government borrows, obviously it increases its debt. Otherwise, Eisner asks, "why else worry about deficits?"

If our incomes grow 4 percent in a year, and prices also rise 4 percent, we are no better or worse off. We have the same "real" purchasing power. If we have $1,000 in a bank account, with 4 percent inflation, that asset will be worth 4 percent less in real purchasing power one year later. It would take 4 percent interest, after taxes, to maintain the real value of the asset. In the same way, if we owe $1,000 and our income rises 4 percent, along with inflation, the real burden of that debt will decline 4 percent in a year.

How does that work for the federal debt and budget deficits? First, keep in mind that the debt is an accumulation of deficits. At the end of fiscal 1989, as I indicated earlier, the debt held by the public is estimated to reach about $2.2 trillion. And if inflation in 1990 averages 4.5 percent, the real value of the $2.2 trillion debt will decline to $2.1 trillion. If the 1990 deficit is about $100 billion, as projected by the 1990 budget, adding that to the debt would bring it back to $2.2 trillion.

In real terms, the debt is unchanged, so that—also in real terms—the budget is balanced. Adding in the $50 billion or so aggregate surplus of state and local governments produces an overall surplus in the government sector.

Professor Eisner contends that fiscal policy, therefore, may be too tight. If we comply with the Gramm-Rudman-Hollings targets which require a balanced federal budget by 1993, we will have, by these kinds of calculations, a huge surplus for the government sector in real terms. "Such a surplus," Eisner claims, "could go far to precipitate a new economic downturn that would make a recession of a few years ago look minor."

Thus, to Eisner, neither the existing debt nor the current budget deficit is an albatross around the economy's neck. On the contrary, he contends that cutting the deficit too much, too quickly, could be an albatross. In this debate, Eisner is among the minority—which, in itself, does not mean he is wrong.

In my opinion, Professor Eisner's view of federal deficits is more accurate than is the view of the debt and deficit doomsayers. His main contribution is in pointing out that a substantial part of government spending is for investment. That's good for the economy. Beyond that, however, his discussion of the effects of changes in government debt on the economy is somewhat overstated. Remember that this government debt also represents assets or wealth to the holders. If this wealth increases, it will stimulate the economy. If it decreases, it will depress the economy—which is what concerns Eisner. But he is over-concerned because these wealth effects have much less than a dollar-for-dollar impact on the economy. The economy hardly blinked after the stock market crash of October 19, 1987.

Second, Eisner does not distinguish between the effects of the federal budget on the economy and the economy on the budget. A lower budget deficit may or may not depress the economy. It *will* if the deficit falls because of reduced spending or increased tax rates. But if economic activity accelerates, for example, because of increased foreign demand for our goods, federal revenues will rise. While that rise might mean some fiscal drag on the economy, it will not signify fiscal tightening. To judge fiscal effects on the economy we should focus on changes in government spending and changes in tax rates.

Eisner's is not a solitary voice in the wilderness, however. Robert Heilbroner and Peter Bernstein have added their support.[8] By adjusting for inflation, capital budgeting, and state and local surpluses, they similarly estimate a $3 billion deficit for 1988. A drop in the bucket, as it were. Their conclusion? If the debt and deficits "were America's No. 1 problem, we would be very well off indeed."

Clearly, viewing the debt and deficits in real terms, there is little to fear from excessive debt. But even in current prices, the total is moderate in relation to the economy. Neither the debt nor the deficits should prompt policymakers to take precipitous actions that might be harmful to the economy in the name of "fiscal responsibility."

In the thirteenth edition of his textbook (economics can be a rewarding profession), Professor Paul Samuelson, with the collaboration of William D. Nordhaus, writes that the debt carries with it three genuine burdens: "the need to service an external debt; the efficiency losses from taxes to pay interest and principal; and the displacement of capital when people hold public debt rather than capital-based assets."[9]

With all due respect to Nobel laureate Paul Samuelson, this argument is weak. On the first point, external debt, he is referring to securities purchased by foreigners. It does not mean that the U.S. government has debt outstanding in a foreign currency over and above its accumulated budget deficits.

The United States has "external debt" only to the extent that foreign residents purchase some of these securities in the open market. At the end of 1988, foreigners held about $350 billion of U.S. treasuries, or 16 percent of the total outstanding. Almost three quarters of those holdings were in foreign official institutions—that is, central banks—accumulated largely for the purpose of stabilizing exchange rates.

---

[8]Robert Heilbroner and Peter Bernstein, *The Debt and the Deficit: False Alarms/ Real Possibilities* (New York: W. W. Norton, 1989).

[9]Samuelson and Nordhaus, *Economics*, p. 400.

Interest on those securities currently amounts to perhaps $30 billion, which comes to six tenths of 1 percent of our GNP. That interest payment does have some minor implications for our balance of payments, but for our overall economy it is not significant.

The authors' second "burden," efficiency losses, is contrived at best. They give an example: "Taxing Paula's interest income or wages to pay Paula interest will introduce microeconomic distortions. Paula may work less hard and may save less. . . ."—presumably as a result of these taxes. I leave it to you to judge the significance of this "loss of efficiency." Do not forget that the economists, politicians, and journalists who complain loudest about our debt generally blame it on President Reagan's tax cuts. Paula was paying more taxes on the same income in 1981 than she did in 1989. If anything, she was working less hard in 1981, when tax rates were much higher.

And third, public debt crowds out private assets. Their explanation: "Let's say for simplicity that people want to hold *a fixed amount* [emphasis added] of wealth in stocks, bonds, real estate and so forth. . . ." Do you know anyone who wants to hold only a fixed amount and no more? Do you think it is true for the country as a whole? If you had heard it before, this might remind you of the old joke about a few people stranded on a tiny desert island. After several days, they find a case of canned foods, but are still in despair because there is no way to open the cans. It turns out, however, that one of them is an economist who announces, "There's no problem, just *assume* a can opener."

Another typical argument for reducing deficits, if not debt, concerns its alleged relationship to our balance of payments. The claim is that we have a foreign trade deficit because we have a budget deficit. A Brookings Institution (in Washington, it is sometimes called "Democrats in Exile") study contains the flat statement that we cannot bring our foreign sector into balance unless we eliminate the budget deficit.[10]

---

[10]Robert E. Litan et al., eds., *American Living Standards* (Washington D.C.: The Brookings Institution, 1988), p. 8.

This is far from an explanation of our foreign balance and, worse, it ignores evidence to the contrary. Sure, the two were in deficit nearly all of the 1980s, but that does not make this a *causal* relationship or a universal truth. During the 1970s, we had budget deficits every year and current account *surpluses* in five years, as we did also in 1980 and 1981. Recently, the United Kingdom shifted into a trade deficit despite a budget surplus while Germany and Japan have huge balance-of-payments surpluses along with budget deficits. And why is the complaint always about the government deficit? How about private borrowing and private debt? Take another look at Chart 3–2.

There is one legitimate reason for reducing our budget deficit, and that is to improve overall economic performance. There is general agreement among economists that we are now (economically) fully employed, and that if the economy grows too rapidly from here on, higher inflation is likely. We need additional resources for real investment and for continued export growth. Reducing the budget deficit might help move the economy toward these desirable goals and away from the lurking dangers.

But cutting the deficit is not the whole answer. It must be done the right way. Simply cutting the deficit will not automatically raise investment in new plant and equipment. We need to free up resources; we also need greater investment incentives and support from the monetary authorities. And we do not have to eliminate the deficit entirely.

Balancing the budget is not a magic elixir that will suddenly cure all our economic viruses, aches, and pains. If we can bring the deficit down to $35 billion to $40 billion in five years, while GNP grows at about a 7-percent nominal rate (including inflation), it would then amount to only about 0.5 percent of the GNP, an acceptable level, in my view.

Most critics of the Reagan administration cite the "Reagan tax cuts" as the cause of the deficits. A little historical perspective might help set the record straight. Actually, Errol Flynn (actor, bon vivant, womanizer), commenting on his own difficulties, prophetically described today's budget situation quite accurately. He is reported to have said once, "My problem lies in reconciling my gross habits with my net income."

Chart 3–1, near the start of this chapter, shows clearly that overspending, not undertaxing, is our gross habit. As late as the mid-1960s, spending and receipts were in the area of 18 percent of GNP. Since then, spending grew much faster than the economy. In 1981, receipts amounted to 20 percent of GNP. The Reagan tax cuts lowered them to about 18 percent again, and now they are about 19 percent.

In the broad sweep of this picture, blaming the deficits on the tax cuts is nonsense or political rhetoric. (Perhaps that's the same thing.) Covering up our gross habit—spending—and blaming it on low taxes, simply lays the groundwork for an increase in taxes—the purpose of which is to feed our gross habit. We need to kick the spending habit and hold the growth in spending to a slower rate than the growth in GNP. If we cannot do this, it will be difficult or impossible to reduce the deficit—*even with a tax increase.*

Admittedly, controlling spending—especially reducing it—is a great deal easier to say than to do. The government establishment will not willingly reduce itself. Every agency in Washington argues strongly, even passionately, in favor of its budget request every year. Within the executive branch, the Office of Management and Budget (OMB) will have to impose across-the-board cutbacks for each department and hold the line.

A similar approach must be taken on the hill to cut back Congress's vast network of committees and staffs, much of which is unnecessary and wasteful. These kinds of measures may save "only" a few billion dollars at first, probably not the tens of billions of dollars needed to make a large dent in the deficit. But as Senator Dirksen once quipped, "a billion here, a billion there, pretty soon it adds up to real money." To achieve any substantial reductions quickly, however, we will have to cut into some of the massive programs or budget sectors.

Chart 3–3 shows the course of some of these large categories in relation to the economy during the past nearly 40 years. While providing some perspectives, this picture may put to rest one myth about spending: Many critics claim that it was a huge jump in defense that drove up total spending. Obviously, defense spending trended downward relative to

CHART 3–3
Major Federal Outlays (As a Percent of GNP)

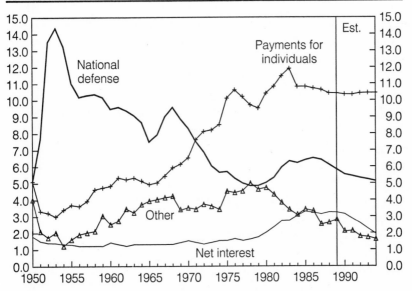

GNP through most of this period, with the exceptions of the Vietnam War years and the Reagan years.

But note that defense spending began to accelerate (relative to the economy) after 1978. Outlays had been cut so sharply after the Vietnam War ended that President Carter proposed a large increase for defense in his last budget message, submitted in early 1981. His projection called for total budget authority of $252 billion for fiscal 1984. Actual spending for that year was held much lower, at $227 billion. And, as the chart indicates, its growth has slowed since then so that it has declined slightly relative to the economy.

The largest spending sector—payments to individuals— was also the fastest growing during this period. In fact, it grew much faster than the economy did. In 1988, these payments reached nearly $500 billion, with social security, income security, and medicare accounting for 86 percent of the total. Growth in outlays for individuals slowed during the 80s, from their increases during the previous decade, a fact for which the Reagan administration came under some criticism.

But this is a "statistical fact," not the actual delivery of services. Inflation eased substantially in the 1980s, accounting for just about all of the slowdown. In real value, with inflation removed, outlays for individuals rose 2.72 percent per year from 1976 to 1980 and 2.64 percent per year from 1980 to 1988—virtually the same rate of increase.

The 1980 to 1983 surge in payments for individuals relative to GNP, represented large increases in outlays as well as little economic growth. During that period, outlays jumped 42 percent, or 12.5 percent per year. The decline in 1984 represents a small further increase in spending and a sharp increase in GNP as the economy rebounded from its recession. Since then, outlays for individuals have settled at 10 to 11 percent of GNP and were projected by the 1990 budget to remain in that range through 1994.

Certainly, if these payments grow in line with the economy, rather than faster as in the previous 35 years or so, it would be easier to deal with the overall budget deficit. Because of the absolute size of this budget sector, politicians occasionally cast a covetous eye on these funds, either for other pet projects or as an easy way to reduce the deficit. A *New Yorker* magazine cartoon once depicted a U.S. senator discussing his proposed legislation with a reporter. It went something like this: "Of course my bill's unfair to the little guy. He's the easiest guy to be unfair to."

Fortunately, the elderly have found ways to band together so that they exert enough political influence to protect their interests. I say "fortunately" because a civilized nation can surely provide legitimate care for its elderly, ill, and disadvantaged; after all, if it can afford tens of billions for "fraud, waste, and abuse," surely it can provide for the less advantaged. Besides, these are legislated programs whose funding is relatively uncontrollable in the federal budget, except by new legislation.

Nonetheless, some savings should be possible in future years with more efficient program management. The Department of Health and Human Services employs about 115,000 people to administer its operations, including social security and medical programs, at a cost of $4 billion to $5 billion per year in direct compensation and supplementary benefits.[11] Without question, a business firm under competitive market conditions, trying to earn a profit, could find ways to deliver the same or even better services with a reduction of 5 to 10 percent of its employees. This would result in savings of several hundred million dollars per year.

More importantly, from a budgetary viewpoint, much more money might be saved by carefully reviewing the methods of payment made to hospitals for medicare and medicaid. This can be done *without* diminishing the existing level of services. Analyses by the Congressional Budget Office (CBO) suggest that such savings might amount to more than $10 billion a year.[12]

The same study by the CBO is even more encouraging with regard to defense spending. Potential savings are enormous, without compromising or cutting into actual defense programs or realistic needs. For starters, take those now infamous, old, inefficient, and/or unnecessary military bases. They remain in operation primarily because they represent Defense Department dollars and jobs for numerous local areas. Not surprisingly, Congressional representatives from those areas have been reluctant to vote them out of existence. And because the bases are distributed around most of the nation, many Congressional votes are involved. Nonetheless, savings from closing or realigning these bases could amount to $3 billion per year,[13] with the added benefit of more efficient operations.

The CBO review covers 31 possible cost-cutting initiatives, each with estimated spending reductions ranging from several hundred million to several billion dollars a year. Some are alternatives to others so that they are not completely additive. Among the "easy ones" are: larger payments by our allies for their defense costs—$3 billion to $4 billion per year;

---

[11]*Budget of the United States Government, Special Analyses, Fiscal Year 1990*, Section I.

[12]Congressional Budget Office, *Reducing the Deficit, A Report to the Senate and House Committees on the Budget-Part II*, February 1989.

[13]Ibid., p. 63.

and reducing the DOD civilian acquisition work force (you know, the ones who buy the $1,000 hammers)—$1 billion to $2 billion per year.

Much larger sums can be saved, of course, in canceling, delaying, or scaling back our large weapons programs. It is certainly not my intention to attempt to evaluate these programs. If we have them and do not need them, they are enormously wasteful. If on rare occasions they preserve our independence and freedom, their value is virtually infinite. And I also believe that having them in sufficient strength has enabled us to avoid using them. But our government leaders must realize that maintaining our national security is no excuse for wasting tens of billions of dollars annually.

A one-year freeze for programs and DOD payrolls, for example, could cut $12 billion a year from the defense budget by 1993,[14] without canceling any weapons systems. One program, however, deserves special attention because of its enormous size. The B-2, or "stealth" bomber is currently our largest single weapons program. Because it is classified, budgetary data are not officially available. But CBO cites press reports that put the total cost at $68 billion. On that basis, they estimate that delaying production and deployment for several years could save $20 billion to $30 billion through 1994,[15] certainly enough to make it a worthwhile consideration.

The comedian Jackie Mason had an even better idea. The B-2 bomber is called "stealth" because its contour or profile does not appear on a radar screen. As Jackie would say—If you cannot see it, we do not have to make it. Just tell the Russians we already have it, it will still be a deterrent, and think of all the money we will save.

Realistically, of course, this would not work; the Russians know almost everything we do. Thus, it may not be possible to hide from them the fact that we do not have the invisible plane.

Another approach might be to include Russia in our foreign aid program. After all, we are providing aid to Poland

---

[14]Ibid., p. 16.
[15]Ibid., p. 47.

and other East European countries. Why not Russia? If we can help their economy to succeed in the free markets and the free world we will have gained a friend and lost an enemy—a net gain of two. The small amount of aid could save many times that amount in defense spending.

Program delays or reductions, however, do not translate automatically into budgetary savings. The Washington establishment does not think that way. The first reaction at the Pentagon would be to hold on to their existing $300 billion budget. If the "stealth" program were cancelled, Pentagon staff would quickly devise new weapons systems to protect against different kinds of threats facing the nation. And I am willing to bet that the new programs proposed would cost about as much as those cancelled. For that reason, cutting defense spending cannot be left to Defense. The Congress will have to "bite the bullet," as it were.

Nor is this mindset unique to DOD. On the contrary, it pervades every agency in the government. And that is why, year in and year out, our government does more things with more people for much more money than the country really needs or wants.

Another area where genuine review is long overdue is agriculture. Its price support, credit, and insurance programs are in need of a major overhaul. As recently as 1976, outlays for these activities totaled $3.2 billion a year. By 1986, the figure had grown to more than $30 billion. "Helped" by the 1988 drought and the resulting price increases, farm subsidies fell to $15 billion. Surely, a program that pays people indefinitely *not* to produce is ridiculous. Yet, this is one of the longest-running shows in town.

The 1990 budget promises to scale back these outlays and encourage the agricultural sector to become more market-oriented and competitive. The administration wants to promote more exports while gradually reducing the domestic price support level. It also proposes shifting from direct federal lending to farmers to guarantees of private loans.

Together with other measures, these changes are expected to reduce agricultural outlays to $10 billion or so in 1993 to 1994, about where they were in 1980 to 1981. If export demand and prices are firm, the cutbacks probably will not be difficult to achieve. If the cutbacks must be achieved mainly by government policy changes, in the face of price weakness, they will not be easy to implement.

My purpose in discussing this material is not to provide an exhaustive menu of possible budgetary savings. That has been done adequately by the CBO and other studies.[16] Rather, it is to argue that substantial savings are possible, even in areas regarded as "untouchable." Achieving these budgetary savings may mean a tough fight against each special interest, but they are certainly worth the effort. The political path of least resistance ordinarily is to keep spending the money.

When political candidates say that they will raise taxes only as a last resort, you should take the threat seriously— they will. They imply that they are wringing all of the waste, inefficiency, and unnecessary activities out of government— they're not. And that is because we, the public, are not pushing our representatives hard enough to do it. They will not do it on their own.

To avoid the painful decisions and responsibilities of specific program cutbacks, the Congress enacted the Balanced Budget and Emergency Deficit Control Act of 1985, popularly known as Gramm-Rudman-Hollings (G-R-H). The act, as amended in 1987, specifies budget deficit limits which decline from $136 billion in fiscal 1989 to $100 billion in 1990, and so on, to a balanced budget in 1993. It also provides a $10 billion leeway for each year, beyond which an automatic sequestration of funds will be required if any *budget* agreed to by the president and the Congress does not fall within the specified limits.

Thus, for 1990, the budget agreed to must provide a deficit of no more than $110 billion. I emphasize *budget* deficit because it is the budget agreement at the beginning of the year that may trigger the G-R-H provisions, not the actual results. For fiscal 1989, the G-R-H target was $136 billion.

---

[16]See especially *The President's Private Sector Survey on Cost Control: A Report to the President, 1984,* (Washington, D.C.: Government Printing Office, 1984).

The actual deficit of $152 billion caused no seqestration. Similarly, if the actual deficit at the end of 1990 exceeds $110 billion, there will be no sequestration.

There are a number of interesting limitations that apply should sequestration be required in any year. First, the entire budget is not subject to sequestration. In fact, almost three quarters of the budget is exempt from these automatic cuts. In the defense area, funds for military personnel and for obligations incurred in prior years are exempt, amounting to 17 percent or so of the total defense budget. In the nondefense portion, well over half is exempt, including social security benefits and low-income programs such as medicaid, family support, child nutrition, and food stamps.

If sequestration were required, it would be applied equally to the nonexempt defense and nondefense areas, but with further limitations. Medicare and health care programs may not be cut more than 2 percent, and the total sequestration may not exceed $36 billion. This does not sound like a huge sum in a $1 trillion budget, but with so much of the budget exempt, the $36 billion could mean average cuts of about 12 percent in the nonexempt areas.

Moreover, if growth in GNP fell below 1 percent at an annual rate for two consecutive quarters, sequestration could be suspended. Such a development seemed remote during the 1982 to 1988 period, when the growth rate averaged over 4 percent per year. But with the economy nearing full employment in 1988 to 1989, our growth probably will not exceed 2.5 percent on average during the early 1990s. A 1 percent growth rate for six months or more during this period would not be unlikely. There is little reason to believe that we may inadvertently have abolished the business cycle.

All of this suggests to me, as it may to you, that G-R-H probably will not eliminate federal deficits by 1993. In addition to all of the exemptions, limits, and escape clauses, the Congress and administration have further leeway; this was described with great clarity by Senator Fritz Hollings:

> The 1990 budget is a spectacular jambalaya of tricks and dodges. For instance, we claim to "save" $2.9 billion by moving

a Pentagon payday from Oct. 1, the new fiscal year, to Sept. 29, in fiscal 1989; and to "cut" another $1.8 billion by moving the Postal Service deficit off-budget (along with the $50 billion-plus cost of bailing out the savings and loan industry.)[17]

And don't forget the real ace up their sleeve: If G-R-H really begins to pinch pet projects, the target dates for balancing the budget can be extended or suspended by new legislation. And you will receive the most reasonable explanations about why it became necessary and why it was beyond their control. They may even tell you why it was the other party's fault.

An honest effort to meet all the targets could even prove self-defeating. Clamping down that hard that quickly on fiscal policy may indeed end this expansion, as Professor Eisner warned, suspending the G-R-H provision and getting both the administration and Congress off the hook.

In a purely mechanical way, we can also try to deal with the budget's red ink with tax increases. Indeed, in the Brookings volume cited earlier, the authors state categorically that "a review of the budget numbers shows that any serious attack on the deficit *must include substantial tax increases* [emphasis added] as well as spending cuts."[18] I suspect that it is their intent to propose higher taxes as a first resort. This proposal reflects simple budgetary arithmetic and probably an ideologic desire to maintain a large government sector. Most of all, it reflects the authors' misguided notion that the budget deficit is our number one problem. The Bible teaches that the reward for the good life is the good life. But fiscal policy for the sake of fiscal policy will not produce good fiscal policy, let alone a good economy. The fact that the 1990 deficit and debt are not historically high when measured against the economy means that we have the time to consider and take steps that will *genuinely* help the economy.

George Bush launched his economic program with the campaign slogan, "Read my lips. No new taxes." The state-

---

[17]Deficit Reduction: A Love Story, *New York Times*, October 25, 1989, p. A31.
[18]Litan et al., *American Living Standards*, p. 8.

ment probably was 99⁴⁴/₁₀₀ percent political, and the rest possibly economic in origin. His campaign manager very likely told him that the public does not want more taxes. Luckily, this campaign promise is consistent with good economic policy.

Given their choice, I suppose the public always will prefer less to more taxes. Why not? Proponents of higher taxes frequently claim that taxes were cut too much and that they are now too low. (Except in times of national emergency, can they ever be *really* too low?) But the facts do not support the claim that taxes are too low—certainly not in historical context. Chart 3–1 showed that total federal receipts in relation to GNP are still relatively high.

Perhaps more meaningfully, Chart 3–4 displays personal tax obligations in relation to taxable personal incomes. The bottom line relates aggregate federal personal income and estate taxes to incomes. In 1988, these taxes amounted to 12 percent of taxable income, down from a peak of 14 percent in 1982, but up from the 10 to 11 percent of the 1960s and early 70s. The middle line relates federal income and estate taxes, plus personal "contributions" (that's what they call it) for social insurance, to the same incomes. The top line is the middle line with the addition of state and local tax and nontax receipts. The taxes included in all three lines are "direct" taxes imposed on individuals. They do not include federal excise taxes or state and local sales taxes—so-called indirect taxes—which can be avoided by not purchasing the taxed items.

The picture supports what you already knew—you are *not* undertaxed. Social security and local taxes have already "made up" for the Reagan income tax cuts. It is difficult to explain what some politicians and economists mean when they tell you your taxes are low. Either they are brainwashed or trying to brainwash you.

And what if your taxes were, in fact, historically low? Would that be bad? It might mean that our government was becoming more efficient in its operations and/or eliminating unnecessary programs. Besides your personal benefits, there are national economic benefits from low taxes. People are encouraged to enter the labor force and to work more if their net reward is higher. Even the high-tax advocates concede this point.

CHART 3–4

Effective Personal Tax Rates—Direct Taxes (Percent of Taxable Income)

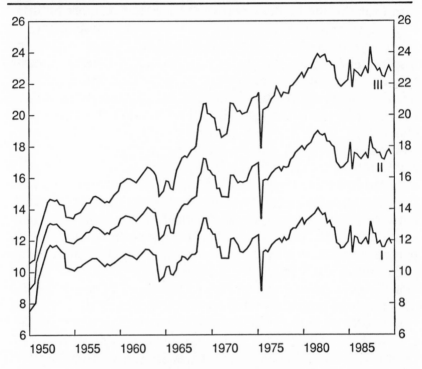

Note: I = Federal income and estate taxes
       II = I + personal contributions for social insurance
       III = Total tax and non-tax receipts, federal, state and local, and
       personal contributions for social insurance.

Part of the incentive to work derives from the fact that the lower the tax rates are, the easier it is for people to accumulate capital. Arthur Okun, the late Brookings economist and Chairman of the Council of Economic Advisers during Lyndon Johnson's presidency, acknowledged that "high tax rates on the affluent" might jeopardize the "rags-to-riches dream."[19]

---

[19]Arthur M. Okun, *Equality and Efficiency* (Washington D.C.: The Brookings Institution, 1975), p. 100.

Raising taxes is also an inefficient way of trying to reduce the budget deficit. A tax increase would tend to slow the economy, which would reduce receipts and offset part of the effects of the higher tax rates. And, perhaps worse, I am completely confident that part of any tax increase would be spent, one way or another, and you would not be able to figure out why. Thus, it would require a larger dollar amount of tax increase than spending cut to achieve the same amount of deficit reduction.

To many people, more tax revenue means, or implies, higher *income* tax rates. As a way around the political impasse of "Read my lips" and Gramm-Rudman requirements, some proposals have been made to "enhance revenues" by using some excise taxes on specific products. These are a tempting, perhaps easier path to take. But they have the same drawbacks as any other taxes and, in one respect, are worse. Surely, the administration cannot accept new excises and claim it has not broken its promise to hold the line on taxes. Besides, it gets the government involved in imposing its value judgments on the public about the desirability, or even morality, of consuming some products.

The CBO estimated that higher taxes on cigarettes, for example, could raise several billion dollars per year in federal revenues. A tax on gasoline similarly could raise substantial revenues coming to about $1 billion per penny per gallon.[20] While I would argue generally against these kinds of taxes, I would also concede that cigarettes are a special case because they are a clear health hazard. Either they should be banned—which, realistically, cannot be done—or heavily taxed to help finance the resulting health costs.

I have more sympathy for raising revenue by eliminating some large preferences and special privileges that the 1986 Tax Reform Act left in place. Taxing credit unions on the same basis as other savings institutions would raise about $1 billion per year; as would the elimination of special preferences for extractive industries (oil, gas, minerals). Further

---

[20]CBO, *Reducing the Deficit,* pp. 361, 371, and 377.

restrictions on deductions for business entertainment could raise $3 billion to $4 billion per year.[21] And the CBO report lists a number of other special items which deserve reconsideration.

One "sacred cow," whose time has come, is the deduction for mortgage interest payments. In fact, I would go further—eliminate *all* interest deductions. These are being phased out for consumers, except for mortgages, but not for corporations. Over the years, these deductions have encouraged borrowing and the buildup of a great amount of private debt, as I showed earlier. Corporations have been encouraged to use debt rather than equity; this tax deduction has facilitated takeovers, many of which are uneconomic, financed by so-called "junk bonds." These bonds, in turn, have been foisted upon an unsuspecting public. *Junk* does not just mean a high rate of interest. It means, in many cases, that the interest and principal will not be paid as promised.

The federal budget documents show that the deduction for mortgage interest payments on owner-occupied homes reduces revenues by $35 billion per year (fiscal 1990 estimate).[22] The important point is not that it "costs the U.S. government" that amount of money. Just who is the U.S. government, and who ultimately pays anyway? The point is that $35 billion is the amount of subsidy given to homeowners, paid for one way or another by those who cannot afford home ownership or who choose to rent. And the payers do not even know it. As with any subsidy, it is unfair to those forced to pay.

The program has a marvelous slogan—it helps our people to achieve the "American dream" of home ownership. The idea, of course, is to help young people get started in life or help anyone who could not afford a home otherwise. If it were limited to that kind of operation, it might not be too bad, although it would still be a subsidy. But note the extent of this tax break: It applies to second homes as well as first and carries a borrowing limit of $1 million. And since Congress

[21]Ibid., pp. 355, 357, 361.
[22]*Special Analyses, Fiscal Year 1990*, p. G-41.

has phased out deductions for interest payments on consumer loans, this deduction enables homeowners to use home equity loans to purchase autos or anything else and still receive the interest deduction.

Viewed against the spirit of "the American dream," these provisions are obscene and at least should be scaled back. The CBO estimates that if the amount of the interest deduction were limited to $12,000 for a single return and $20,000 for a joint return, government revenues would be raised about $2 billion a year.[23] Alternatively, if the *tax saving* from the deduction were limited to 15 percent of the interest paid (the tax rate of the lowest bracket), the budget would pick up an additional $10 billion a year in 1990, growing to almost $13 billion in 1994.

If the Congress were to begin hearings on any of these changes, one can imagine the intensity of the opposition lobbying that would be brought to bear by groups of home-builders, realtors, bankers, and perhaps a few homeowners. Frankly, I do not think the Congress has the guts to make any of these changes. But should we be pleasantly surprised, and they enact these or similar limitations on benefits, I would not recommend using the additional revenues for deficit reduction. Cutting back the subsidies would translate into reduced building activity. Thus, we would have more real resources available for the rest of economy. If we then also had the courage to enact new, genuine investment incentives, these resources could be shifted toward the production of more plant and equipment.

The Bush administration has taken a (small) step in this direction in proposing a lower tax rate for capital gains. As with any important fiscal change, the proposal immediately aroused both political opposition and support. One of the main issues in the ensuing debate concerned the impact this measure would have on receipts and the budget deficit. President Bush's staff, armed with figures from the Treasury Department's Office of Tax Analysis, maintained that a lower capital gains rate would *raise* revenues. Opponents in the Congress

---

[23]CBO, *Reducing the Deficit,* p. 321.

claimed that the lower rates would *lower* revenues and raise the deficit; to support their claim, they used Treasury Department analyses prepared two years earlier which estimated a higher deficit.

Based on existing market transactions, the direct effect of the rate reduction would lower revenues and raise the deficit. The net effect, then, turns on whether the lower rates would encourage more asset sales, thereby raising revenues. The Treasury Department claims it would. A study by Patric Hendershott and Yunhi Won concludes that the long-run net effect would be a larger deficit.[24] On a long-run basis, I believe that Hendershott and Won are correct.

One of the compromise proposals offered would limit the lower rates to a two- or three-year period. If that were done, revenues would rise during that period. But what would a two-year measure do for the economy? Probably nothing or very little. I come back, therefore, to a point I raised earlier, and that is the folly of fiscal policy for the sake of fiscal policy. Using this measure to avoid or lessen Gramm-Rudman sequestration in 1990 and/or 1991 is pure politics.

Another issue that has been raised in opposition to lower capital gains rates concerns who will receive the tax benefit. There is little doubt that it will be people in the highest income brackets. They are the ones with the capital.

Senator Bill Bradley, an original sponsor of tax reform, argued that "If they put a loophole back in that will largely benefit people earning $200,000 or more a year, we should have a higher tax rate for those individuals."[25] Calvin Trillin, the humorist, added that he has finally come to understand the meaning of supply-side economics: "We have a limited supply of rich people, so we have to take good care of them."[26]

To offset the benefit of the lower capital gains rate, Senator Bradley would raise the income tax rate for the

---

[24]Patric Hendershott and Yunhi Won, "The Long-Run Impact on Federal Revenues and Capital Allocation of a Cut in the Capital Gains Tax," NBER Working Paper No. 2962, 1989.

[25]"Bradley Says He'd Back a Tax Hike for Wealthy if Capital Gains Levy Is Cut." As quoted by Robert Cohen in the New Jersey *Star-Ledger*, September 22, 1989, p. 9.

[26]Ibid., October 9, 1989, p. 16.

highest income group from 28 percent to 33 percent, thereby maintaining a progressive rate structure. But the Tax Reform Act of 1986 already increased the degree of progressivity. Samuelson and Nordhaus show that the act *raised* taxes 3 percent for households with incomes in the highest 10 percent group, while *lowering* taxes 44 percent for households in the lowest 10 percent group. Changes for the other income deciles range smoothly between these extreme values.[27] Therefore, the question of who gets the benefit of this tax break should be viewed against the backdrop of the entire tax structure. In any case, this should not be the main issue.

The main issue concerning the capital gains tax rate has not been debated at all. That is the effect of this measure on new real investment. The questions about whether the lower capital gains rate would raise or reduce the budget deficit and about which income group would get the tax break are close to irrelevant. Virtually the only comments about the effects on real investment have come from the Bush administration. And their claims that investment would be greatly increased are greatly exaggerated.

According to the Bureau of Economic Analysis econometric model, the effect would be small. If the maximum rate on capital gains were lowered permanently to 15 percent, business fixed investment would rise $45 billion (in constant 1982 prices) during the next 10 years. That is about $4.5 billion per year, amounting to well under one percentage point added growth to real investment—a puny amount but better than nothing.

A second projection was made on the basis of a 20 percent reduction in the "tax lives" for producers' durable equipment. That would permit faster depreciation write-offs and larger tax deductions as a result of investment. The model says that enacting this provision would raise real investment $89 billion over ten years, or 1.5 percent per year. A third projection was based on reinstatement of the 10 percent investment tax credit for equipment. And this provision was the grand winner, adding $368 billion of new investment

---

[27]Samuelson and Nordhaus, *Economics*, p. 794.

(again in constant 1982 prices) over 10 years, or 5.5 percent a year. In current prices, the gain would be over $700 billion in total, or $70 billion per year.

Critics might complain, however, that we cannot afford it, because a 10 percent investment tax credit would raise the federal budget deficit $30 billion a year. But that trade-off— $70 billion per year in new investment for $30 billion in budget deficits—would be an excellent bargain. Our public servants in Washington, in this case, the U.S. Treasury, can borrow money at an interest cost of 8 to 9 percent, while the additional investment in plant and equipment would earn a nominal return of about twice that rate and probably more.[28]

If there is a problem, it is not financial or budgetary—it is real resources. And there may be some irony here yet. At economically full employment, we may not be able to add $70 billion a year to the economy, even for new investment. That is, we may not have enough capacity to produce the new equipment that would expand our capacity and raise the economy's growth potential. "Too little, too late," as they used to say early in the Great War.

If we ever come to an enlightened fiscal policy, our leaders will move to raise or maintain high levels of investment well before our industrial operating rates reach 80 percent of capacity. At today's 82 to 83 percent, some scattered inflationary pressures already have appeared. If the capital gains provision were implemented for only two or three years, it would have virtually no effect on real investment. In that regard, it would not be better than nothing. It probably would encourage Wall Street profit-taking and thereby raise budget revenues initially. But it would reduce them later and reduce them over a long period of time.

The trouble with our fiscal or budget policy is that it is not policy, it is politics. I cannot put it any better than Senator George Mitchell, the Democratic Majority Leader, did: "We expend so much energy and effort here seeking to get and retain partisan advantage that we lose focus on dealing with

---

[28]George N. Hatsopoulos, Paul R. Krugman, and Lawrence H. Summers, "U.S. Competitiveness beyond the Trade Deficit," *Science,* July 15, 1988, p. 305.

legislation in a responsible way."[29] If the only thing that matters is reducing the deficit, that's fine. But as a nation, we have needs and should have priorities; these would suffer from across-the-board cuts. Nonetheless, I prefer Gramm-Rudman to raising taxes, and I prefer it to not cutting spending at all.

In the good old days, (from the point of view of the government, that would be before 1981) we used to be able to inflate our way out of budget deficits. As incomes rose along with inflation, individuals found themselves moving into higher and higher tax brackets. The result was that revenues rose faster than inflation and faster than incomes. Thus, individuals suffered annual tax increases, and the government enjoyed rising revenues to support its spending habit without the need to legislate higher taxes.

One of the most important fiscal accomplishments of the Reagan administration was to end this travesty through "indexing" individuals' tax brackets for inflation. Now if the Congress wants to push people into higher tax brackets, they will have to go on record and vote for it. They can no longer hide behind the skirts of inflation. Inflation will still raise revenue, however, by raising incomes. But the rates remain the same from year to year. The increase in tax revenue, therefore, will be in proportion to the rise in incomes, not in an ever increasing proportion.

Another reason that we can no longer inflate our way out of the deficit is that many of our large spending programs are indexed for inflation and therefore rise at least as fast as inflation. These include government pensions and the huge social security program. Other programs are raised also by inflation, without indexing, as their costs rise.

The net effect of inflation on the budget, therefore, is small. Analysis of budget sensitivity to economic assumptions shows that a one percentage point rise in inflation (and

---

[29]A Deal Offered on Tax Bill, *New York Times,* October 6, 1989, p. D1. I did not select this passage for partisan purposes. A Republican senator or White House staffer might have said the same thing. Senator Mitchell should be congratulated for his honesty.

interest rates right along with it—a not unreasonable assumption) would add marginally to the deficit—about $1 billion to $2 billion a year.[30]

But real growth is quite another matter. The effects all shift in the same direction. Similar analysis shows that a sustained one percentage point lower annual growth rate in GNP, with correspondingly higher unemployment (and unemployment benefits), would raise the budget deficit by more than $80 billion within 5 years; and conversely, for faster growth. No wonder the Bush administration is leaning on Alan Greenspan, the Chairman of the Federal Reserve Board, to ease monetary policy and promote faster economic growth.

Richard Darman, Director of the OMB, apparently is the president's "designated hitter" in criticizing the Fed's monetary tightness and arguing *publicly* for lower interest rates and faster monetary growth. Using a public forum is playing politics. Senior White House officials meet frequently with Mr. Greenspan and make their views known to him. Going public simply means that should a recession occur before November 1992, the White House will try to blame Mr. Greenspan for it and hope to avoid any political harm to Mr. Bush and to Republican Congressional candidates.

You may be confident also that Mr. Darman was not speaking out on his own or only for himself. These things are planned at meetings of the Cabinet and the Economic Policy Council. Besides, the president apparently knew of it in advance, as he could then support Darman's comments publicly: "I can feel very comfortable with his 'sallying forth' and saying that."[31] *("Sallying forth?")*

The trouble is that, at near-full employment, more monetary stimulation would mean slightly more real growth and probably a good deal more inflation. And while this combination would improve the budget deficit and help the administration in its political skirmishes with the Congress, it would

---

[30]*Budget of the United States Government, Fiscal Year 1990*, p. 3-25.
[31]Economic Scene, *New York Times*, August 18, 1989, p. D2.

be harmful to the economy. Mr. Greenspan's responsibility is the economy, not Mr. Bush's reelection. Is there no way out of this dilemma? Only if we could accelerate economic growth without also raising inflation. Well, we *can* do that—you have already heard my argument: more resources shifted into investment.

Interestingly, Mr. Darman paid some lip service to this issue in a well-publicized speech in mid-1989: "In our public policy—as, to some degree, in our private behavior—we consume as though there were no tomorrow. We attend too little to the issues of investment necessary to make tomorrow brighter."[32]

Other Washington figures have gone through the motions of criticizing excessive consumption and deficient investment. It goes with the territory. But at least Mr. Darman included government excesses and did not limit his criticism to those of private individuals. He has also acknowledged that government tax provisions encourage corporate debt rather than equity financing.

Fine, Mr. Darman, now how about translating these sentiments into actions? We have to eliminate the tax deductions—corporate and individual—for interest payments, including at least part of the interest on mortgages. Because existing debt was incurred with the understanding that interest cost was tax-deductible, the change should apply to new borrowing. But it will not take forever to implement the new provision. The average life of a mortgage is around 11 years; so after that time, the portion still carrying tax-deductible interest may be under 25 percent.

To the extent that the tax change would succeed in reducing private borrowing, it would lower interest rates. And you can lower personal income tax rates further to offset the ensuing rise in revenue. Surely consumers as a group would not be hurt by that package. They would work more and save more, just as you asked. And the lower interest rates, of course, would lower the budget deficit.

---

[32]The Nation, *New York Times,* July 30, 1989, p. E4.

You also argue for more investment—at least that is what I think you meant when you said, "We attend too little to the issues of investment." Need I remind you, Mr. Darman, that you were Deputy Secretary of Treasury when your department prepared the tax reform bill that knocked out the investment incentives? Not that it was necessarily your fault. In fact, I think that the provision was introduced while Don Regan was at Treasury and you were still at the White House. You should reintroduce the Investment Tax Credit.

If a 10 percent credit frightens you because it would "cost" $30 billion a year in revenue, then go for 5 percent. It would still be better than your silly capital gains rate and by a wide margin. And don't raise corporate taxes on earnings to pay for the investment tax credit. You raised corporate taxes in 1986; besides, you will be eliminating interest deductions. On balance, you should be lowering corporate taxes.

There is one more change in the tax structure that would be beneficial to the economy, Mr. Darman. I hesitate to mention it because it probably doesn't stand a snowball's chance in Washington—that is a value-added tax. (To the reader: This form of tax, known as VAT, would work something like a national sales tax.)

I know that the opposition will scream that it is regressive. But we can exempt food, clothing, and rent, and it can be blended with the income tax system. The great advantages are that a VAT does not tax and discourage work and earnings; it taxes consumption, thus encouraging saving.

Another advantage of a VAT is that it would make us more price competitive in foreign trade. The General Agreement on Tariffs and Trade (GATT) permits the rebate of any VAT to exporters, who can then lower their prices. All of the major European countries and Japan use VATs as part of their overall tax system and use them to enhance their foreign trade balance. (End of comments to Mr. Darman or his successor.)

Not long ago, two Nobel laureates in economics, Franco Modigliani and Robert Solow, wrote a letter to the editor of the *New York Times*. They took issue with Robert Eisner's argument that, in real terms, the budget deficit was very small and that if we actually were to adhere to the Gramm-

Rudman targets, we might throw the economy into recession. One important point of contention concerns our trade deficit. They wrote:

> What he [Eisner] fails to realize is that none of his proposed solutions will reduce the trade deficit, unless we free resources to be used for more net exports. This requires that we either cut the [budget] deficit or cut investment. Failure to do so under conditions of full, if not overfull, employment would threaten to overload the economy, courting the risk of serious inflation. Most thoughtful people agree that cutting investment is the last thing we should consider—This leaves cutting the deficit as the *only* [emphasis added] acceptable option.[33]

For two Nobel laureates, I find their statement naive and disappointing. They express concern over the availability of resources for future growth now that our economy is at full employment—that's fine. And they argue against cutting investment—that's great. Then they are left with cutting the federal deficit as the *only* means of freeing resources—that's wrong. What about consumer spending, homebuilding, and state and local activity? Besides, the federal deficit, *per se,* does not use *real* resources. Federal *spending,* directly and indirectly, uses resources—22 to 23 percent-worth.

"If someone came down from Mars and looked at our economic problems, they would be amazed at how much attention we pay to the deficit," admitted Charles Schumer, Democratic Congressman from Brooklyn and a consummate politician who has criticized our budget deficits. "What it [the deficit] is really is a security blanket. When things go wrong, you can always blame it on the deficit. Other problems are more serious but the deficit is easier to talk about."[34]

There is no issue or problem that politicians do not attempt to turn to partisan advantage. But the budget deficit may be doing some good. Milton Friedman, one of the first American Nobel laureates in economics, observed that the deficit *was* restraining spending, even among Democratic

---

[33]Letter to the Editor, *New York Times,* March 12, 1989.
[34]Why the Deficit Is Paralyzing Congress *New York Times,* October 22, 1989, p. E1.

Congressmen. Without the deficit, spending probably would still be climbing as a share of the economy. To help you distinguish between Milton Friedman and Benjamin Friedman, think of Milton as the *right* Friedman and Benjamin as the *wrong* Friedman.

Eisner had pointed out that just cutting the budget deficit would not automatically raise private investment. That assumption "is a gigantic leap of faith. If our disposable [i.e., after tax] income were reduced . . . so that we decided not to buy that new Chrysler, would Lee Iacocca be likely to invest in more plants, or fewer?"[35] Undoubtedly fewer.

Eisner is right. If we were to tighten up sufficiently on fiscal policy, the economy would go into recession. The recession would lower the trade deficit by reducing imports. That cure would be worse than the disease (a metaphor economists like to use). Maybe that is not what Modigliani and Solow had in mind, but that is what their recommendations would accomplish.

Eisner's alternative proposal is to lower the dollar to stimulate our exports and discourage imports by making them more costly. That approach to improving the trade deficit is preferable to a recession, but it is not our best alternative. It has disadvantages including higher inflation. We can do better than that. We need to improve our basic economic performance, especially to achieve faster growth in productivity. That would help to cut costs. And the better we perform in this regard, the less the dollar needs to fall in order to make us competitive in foreign trade.

So I come back to the advice I offered earlier. With sincerest apologies to Dylan Thomas, "Do not go gentle into" new taxes. "Rage, rage against" waste in government. Invest your money in your own businesses. It will be good for you and good for your country. Leave it to our politicians in Washington to fight out the budget battle on the spending side. If it takes longer than five years, that's fine. They deserve it.

---

[35]Letter to the Editor, *New York Times,* February 19, 1989.

Chapter Four

INTERNATIONAL TRADE AND FOREIGN INVESTMENT
REDUCTIO AD ABSURDUM

> **Myths:** 1. Our foreign trade deficits are killing us. 2. We're now completely "hooked" on foreign capital to finance our budget deficit and our economy.
> **Facts:** The first claim is greatly exaggerated; the second is wrong.

Probably no area in economics is as misunderstood and confusing as the international sector. International trade and investment represent a great many vested interests: business gained through exports, business lost through imports, increased foreign ownership of assets in the United States, and growing competition from foreign-owned firms with production facilities in the United States. Because they are so easily misunderstood, international trade and investment lend themselves readily to political and economic demagoguery. As a result, these have become two of the most misrepresented areas in economics.

As often as not, our foreign trade is discussed under the heading *Foreign Trade Problem.* Yes, we do have a deficit, and—despite its shrinkage since 1987—the deficit is still large. Nonetheless, international trade in general is not a problem. Nor is it a goal or end in itself. Our real goal is economic growth, to provide rising incomes and thereby a rising standard of living for our people.

Our foreign trade, in deficit or surplus, can help us toward that goal because it gets us things we do not have at home. We can buy many things cheaper and/or better than we can make them. And, if conducted reasonably freely and fairly, foreign trade encourages us to do the things that we do best relative to other countries. This is what economists refer to as "comparative advantage." Trade, therefore, certainly contributes to global well-being, including our own.

Ben Franklin once said that no nation was ever ruined by trade. Perhaps the benefits were clearer at that time when we were a developing nation, trading our agricultural products for European manufactured goods. If the benefits are not as obvious now that we are the world's leading industrial as well as agricultural nation, they are still just as real and just as great. Our main trading partners today are the other industrial nations; and, as such, they are also our competitors. The process of competition promotes efficiency for all of us by causing each country to specialize in the areas of its greatest relative efficiency or unique products.

Of course, competition means hard work, and therefore it is not the most widely supported approach to trade. Protection is easier. A century and a half ago, Thomas Babington, Lord Macauley, observed that "Free trade, one of the great blessings which a government can confer on a people, is in almost every country unpopular."

And so it is today. But then just as now, each country was schizophrenic in its view of foreign trade. Producers and consumers always have had opposing views. Of the two groups (admittedly, they are not mutually exclusive), the producers (usually a minority) are the ones who make their views known to government officials. During my tenure in Washington, I remember clearly the stream of individuals representing businesses, industries, and trade associations, looking for protection from fair as well as unfair competition. It is much easier to grow fat and lazy than to compete, but protection will not make our economy any better.

Maybe there were representatives of consumer groups also, but I do not recall them. I cannot recall any objections voiced by Ralph Nader, for example, when Japanese auto producers were asked, to the detriment of American consumers, to limit their exports to the United States. The limited supply of imported cars meant less competition, more domestic assemblies and higher prices to all consumers. Auto workers are among the highest paid in United States manufacturing, so that the quotas forced workers in other industries to subsidize the higher-paid auto workers.

"The end of all commerce," wrote David Riccardo early last century, "is to increase production, and that, by increasing production, though you may occasion partial loss, you increase the general happiness."[1] That commerce increases the general happiness, or welfare, is beyond question. And that is the fundamental argument in favor of encouraging more world trade.

Okay, we can all agree that foreign trade is good for us in theory. But what happens in practice when we open our markets to imports, and others maintain barriers against our goods and subsidize their exporters to help them gain a larger share of U.S. and world markets? What happens when foreign investors and speculators buy dollars and dollar assets in such quantity that they drive the exchange value of the dollar well above the point where it reflects trade relationships and the prices of internationally traded goods? What happens when our economy grows very rapidly, as it did after 1982, and the economies of our trading partners grow much more slowly and largely by exporting to the United States? And what happens when some of our best customers—Mexico and other Latin American countries—run into debt problems and have to cut imports in order to maintain a trade surplus and be able to pay interest on foreign loans?

What happens is what *happened*. We ran up a big foreign trade deficit. In 1980, we had a shortfall of $25 billion. But

---

[1]David Riccardo, *The Principles of Political Economy and Taxation*, Everyman's Library, No. 590, New York: E.P. Dutton, London: J. M. Dent & Sons Ltd., 1955, p. 181.

that was more than covered by a large surplus in the service accounts—mainly investment income from abroad—so that the overall "current account" was in surplus. By 1987, two years after the dollar peaked, the merchandise trade deficit crested at $160 billion. The surplus in services had shrunk also, so that the balance on current account showed a deficit of $144 billion.

The growing trade deficit meant that more and more of the goods we were buying were produced abroad. We were losing increasing amounts of business output, jobs, and incomes—at least through 1987 when the deficit peaked. Nonetheless, our economy continued to grow and by 1988 to 1989, most economists agree that we were approaching full employment, with foreign trade still in deficit. This meant that output and jobs had shifted on balance, to other areas of the economy, away from manufacturing toward services.

The four factors cited—foreign barriers against our exports, the runup in the dollar, relatively rapid growth in the United States, and Latin American debt problems—account for all, or nearly all, of the rise in our trade deficit. However, they were not equally important, and not all of them can be considered adverse developments. Trade barriers existed throughout the period; but I doubt that these barriers contributed to more than 10 percent of the increase in the trade deficit.

However, Congressman Dick Gephart, Democrat of Missouri, discovered that foreign barriers were a marvelous political issue on which he could promote his career. He even campaigned for the presidential nomination in 1988 on this issue. He also introduced legislation in the House to deal with this matter—a retaliatory, protectionist trade bill. Had the bill become law, we would have ended up in a trade war with our allies. This would have hurt our own consumers and probably cost us many jobs. Ultimately, it would have torn up world trade severely to the detriment of us all. Fortunately, Mr. Gephart lost in both his quests. His party rewarded him, however, with appointment as Majority Whip to succeed Tony Coelho who had resigned to avoid a Congressional inquiry into his possible wrongdoings.

Our relatively rapid economic growth did raise the deficit, but this was hardly an adverse development. After all, we are concerned about the deficit because it represents lost business and lost jobs, at least in some sectors. Thus, cause and effect in this relationship were reversed—from the economy to the trade balance. Our economy was growing rapidly, so we imported more goods—both raw materials for our production processes and finished goods to satisfy rising domestic demand. Our trading partners maintained sluggish growth, so our exports to them lagged behind what they should have been. Certainly, this imbalance between our growth and theirs required some adjustment on the part of our trading partners.

Reagan administration officials prodded Germany in particular to pick up the pace. They were the European economic engine; they had high unemployment, no inflation, and a huge trade surplus—all signs of an economy calling for faster growth. But they moved slowly, citing their traditional fear of inflation.

Debt problems of Latin American countries also hurt our exports. The financially strapped countries had taken loans in foreign currencies, mainly dollars. (This is a major difference between their debt and what is generally referred to loosely as our "debt.") As a result, in order to pay our banks interest in dollars, they cut their imports from the United States. Our exports to these countries dropped from $43 billion in 1981 to $26 billion in 1983. From there, they began a slow recovery, but did not reach the $43 billion level again until 1988.

Some international lenders, both official and private institutions, have argued that these countries must tighten their belts. But asking low-income people to adopt measures of austerity is ridiculous; and it is detrimental to our economy. A better solution is to increase economic growth among the industrial countries and expand world trade; this would raise LDC exports and incomes.

That brings us to the dollar; and this factor alone probably accounted for more than half the rise in the trade deficit. From its low point in the fall of 1980 to its peak in the spring of 1985, the dollar rose some 50 percent, on average, against the other major currencies. In addition, our domestic inflation added 25 percent or so to the prices of our goods. To foreign purchasers of U.S. products, the combined increases represented an enormous price hike. It's no wonder that our products, including agricultural ones, lost so many of their key foreign markets.

At the same time, foreign goods became cheaper to Americans, although by proportionately less than the drop in their currencies relative to the dollar. Because the dollar is the main international currency, many items manufactured abroad are priced in dollars when they are shipped into the world markets. By reducing prices less than the declines in their currencies, foreign producers simultaneously increased their business and widened their profit margins.

Our rapid growth and the strength of the dollar helped our foreign competitors achieve major gains in U.S. markets. From 1982 to 1987, U.S. merchandise imports jumped by two thirds, for an average of 11 percent per year. The drop in oil prices in 1985 and 1986 helped slow the tide. During those five years, imports of nonpetroleum products, mainly manufactured goods, *doubled.*

At the same time, our exports barely held their own. From 1982 to 1985, they gained a meager 2 percent. U.S. exports responded well, however, to the dollar's sharp drop of nearly one half from early 1985 to the end of 1987. They jumped 12 percent in 1987 and a whopping 28 percent in 1988.

Perhaps you noticed that in discussing the merchandise trade deficit and its causes, I have not even mentioned the budget deficit. In the preceding chapter, I cited a Brookings paper and a letter by Professors Modigliani and Solow, which virtually *equated* budget and trade deficits. Equating them greatly exaggerates their relationship. Do we buy more foreign goods or sell less goods abroad just *because* we have a budget deficit or a *larger* budget deficit? That, I assure you, does not make economic sense, let alone common sense.

Perhaps we can make some sense of it through indirect relationships. Of the four causal factors I cited, two are fundamental economic determinants—economic growth and the exchange value of the dollar. Economists refer to the first as an *income effect* and to the second factor—the dollar—as a *price effect.*

Did the budget deficit contribute to the trade deficit? It probably did; but certainly not on a dollar-for-dollar basis. The tax cuts of the early 1980s contributed importantly to the economic pickup. However, many people think that monetary policies also played a role in the strong growth of 1982 to 1988.

Similarly, the higher budget deficits may have contributed to the rise in the dollar, but this is difficult to quantify. The argument is that the budget deficits increased Treasury borrowing and raised interest rates which then attracted more funds from foreign investors, thereby boosting the dollar.

But the events do not entirely support this thesis. Interest rates rose from 1982 to 1984, but that is normal during an expansion period; and rates declined between 1984 and 1986 as the budget deficit was reaching its peak. The federal budget is not the sole determinant of interest rates, and probably not the major determinant. There are other key factors: the strength of private credit demands, inflation, and Federal Reserve policies.

Econometricians who have tried to model the relationship between Treasury borrowing and interest rates have met with mixed results. Besides, the dollar peaked in early 1985, and its decline followed the pattern of the interest rates—not the budget deficits.

There are also key reasons, other than interest rates, that foreigners have elected to invest in the United States. These include a basically healthy economy with good prospects for long-term gains in earnings; the improved investment incentives, which raised the returns to capital, at least prior to the Tax Reform Act of 1986; political uncertainties in Germany, Japan and other countries; and the United States' traditional role as a safe haven for foreign funds. Certainly, we cannot lay the blame for the trade deficit solely at the feet of the budget. Evidence reveals that the relationship between trade and budget deficits was almost nonexistent before 1980 in the United States; and it is nonexistent today in other countries.

One more explanation of our merchandise trade deficit is worth mentioning, to inject a lighter note, if for nothing else. The Congressional Budget Office (CBO), which provided the extensive survey of possible budget savings, also produced a paper on our trade deficit. Listen to this statement: "A good way to *understand why* [emphasis added] the United States has a large current-account deficit," which is now virtually the same as our trade deficit, "is to look at the discrepancy between its production and its expenditures."[2]

But that is what a trade deficit *is*. When imports exceed exports, our expenditures exceed our production. If we exported more than we imported, our production would exceed our expenditures. But *how* do you get there? Their explanation is the same as saying that we have a trade deficit because we import more than we export; or about as useful as saying that the stock market rose because "there were more buyers than sellers."

Whatever its causes, and it is clear there are several important ones, the trade deficit has reduced U.S. output. But general agreement on this point is no license to exaggerate it. In late 1988, a Washington think tank—the Economic Policy Institute—released a report purporting to show that the trade deficit of $170 billion in 1987 (later redefined to $160 billion) "cost the country 5.1 million jobs."[3]

Martin Crutsinger, a knowledgeable Associated Press reporter, called me to discuss the report. I took the opportunity to observe that total unemployment in the economy at that time amounted to only 6.6 million and that we could not add 5 million more jobs. That would lower our unemployment rate to 1 percent. Switzerland can do that—we cannot. What

---

[2]Congressional Budget Office, *Policies for Reducing the Current-Account Deficit,* August 1989, p. xi.
[3]AP wire service report, October 5, 1988.

happened is that many of the people who lost jobs because of the trade deficit found new jobs in other areas of the economy. The Economic Policy Institute, a "labor-backed" group with an ax to grind, responded that the Labor Department figures understate unemployment.[4] In effect, "our minds are made up; do not confuse us with the facts." They then held a luncheon meeting to present their findings. And guess who was the discussion leader—Dick Gephart.

What the institute really is complaining about is that the trade deficit—which affects mainly the manufacturing sector—has resulted in a shift away from some union jobs in manufacturing to more nonunion jobs in other areas. In their defense, they are not the only research group with a vested interest in their studies and findings.

I agree completely, however, that the trade deficit means lost business, at least in some industries. Reducing it by increasing exports and by recapturing domestic markets will raise economic activity, especially in the affected industries.

Now let's move on to the second part of the chapter heading—foreign investment in the United States. Consider this statement: "Without the funds from abroad, the U.S. rate of net investment in housing and in plant and equipment this year would have been cut in half and interest rates would have gone through the roof."[5] And this one:

> In 1987 foreign funds financed 22 percent of the gross investment undertaken in America. If these were to be withdrawn, 22 percent of the machine tools could not be purchased, 22 percent of the new homes could not be built and 22 percent of the industrial and commercial construction would have to be cancelled. ... America's addiction to foreign funds is your most troubling short-term problem.[6]

---

[4]Ibid.

[5]Martin Feldstein, "The End of Policy Coordination," *The Wall Street Journal,* November 9, 1987, p. 26.

[6]Lester C. Thurow, "A Briefing for the Next President," *New York Times,* August 21, 1988, Business section.

The first statement was by Martin Feldstein, a Harvard professor and a former Chairman of the Council of Economic Advisers, and the second by Lester Thurow, Dean of the School of Management at MIT. Great credentials, right? But they're both dead wrong! Similarly, the Brookings paper cited earlier, also contains references to our "dependence on foreign creditors."[7] And so do many other discussions. In fact, I think this is the view of the majority of economists. What's wrong with it?

Foreign countries do not print dollars or create dollar balances through their central banks. Only the U.S. Federal Reserve System does that. If a foreign investor wishes to obtain dollars, he can buy them from other foreign holders or from Americans. In the first case, there is no change in total foreign holdings; in the second, there is an increase in foreign holdings, which we call an "inflow of capital." But note that in the second case there is a corresponding increase in American holdings of foreign currencies. In neither case is there a *net* inflow of foreign capital.

Nor do I think that the expression *inflow of capital* is accurate. If foreigners obtain dollar balances from Americans, what happens is that the ownership of the dollars is transferred to foreigners. While we call it an inflow, they do not actually ship dollars here. But in the process of buying dollars, they bid up the dollar's foreign exchange value.

In the end, foreigners accumulate more assets here than we gain abroad through our trade deficit. When we buy their goods and services, we pay them dollars. (The process is the same when we pay in foreign currencies that we have to purchase for U.S. dollars.) When they buy goods and services from us, they pay us dollars. Since we import more goods than we export, they end up with a net increase in dollars. Thus, while we call their net accumulation of dollars "capital inflow," they do not actually send capital. What do they send? They send goods.

---

[7]Robert E. Litan et al., eds., *American Living Standards* (Washington, D.C.: The Brookings Institution, 1988), pp. 10, 11, etc.

By sending (or, more accurately, selling) goods here, they earn income here. By buying less here than they sell, they save part of that income. That saving is the source of their net accumulation of capital here. And that saving has the same effect on our economy as saving by U.S. residents. A rise in saving, *in itself,* tends to slow down the economy. Conversely, an increase in consumption of U.S. goods by U.S. residents or by foreigners tends to speed up the growth of the U.S. economy.

Which brings me back to the title of this chapter—International Trade and Foreign Investment. This is not a two-for-one bargain offer or a matter of killing two subjects with one chapter. Trade, or trade imbalances, and (net) foreign investment are opposite sides of the same coin.

Every quarter, the Commerce Department's Bureau of Economic Analysis (BEA) publishes data on U.S. international transactions in their *Survey of Current Business.* For any quarter or year, the net foreign investment or net inflow of capital (net of outflow) is equal to the U.S. Balance on Current Account—except for a statistical discrepancy incurred in gathering data for the almost innumerable transactions. The two measures, current account balance and net capital inflow, are identically equal by definition and roughly equal statistically.

A similar observation may be made about the stock market. One frequently hears the comment that money is "flowing into the market," or "flowing out of the market." As with the U.S. capital inflow from abroad, those comments are literally incorrect. If I were to buy 100 shares of XYZ Corporation from you at $10 per share, my $1,000 has not flowed into the market. You now have the $1,000. It flowed into your pocket. The only way, literally, that we can have a net inflow of money to the stock market is when XYZ or another Corporation issues new securities to the public. The amount of issue, net of brokerage fees, is the net amount of money flowing into the market. In this case, the inflow is equal to the amount of corporate external financing.

But even if there were no new corporate securities issued for some period of time, this would not mean that market transactions for existing securities would not affect their prices. On the contrary, these transactions are what drive market prices. What matters to prices, or price changes, is which side—demand or supply—initiates the transaction.

The same is true for the foreign exchange value of the dollar, with regard to both the price of the dollar and the question of capital inflow. As long as the current account is in balance, there is no net inflow of capital. The net inflow of capital rises and falls with the current account deficit. Nonetheless, we hear two arguments simultaneously: first, that the trade deficit (which accounts now for virtually all of the current account deficit) is depressing our economy, and second (for example, Feldstein and Thurow cited above), that the inflow of foreign capital is financing our budget deficit and much of our investment. In effect, foreign capital allegedly is financing our growth. Surely, if real investment were cut in half, our economy would fall into a severe recession.

But both of these arguments cannot be right. If they were, they would be saying, in effect, that the trade deficit is both depressing our economy and stimulating our economy. Reductio ad absurdum. Which argument is right? The first one, of course. When in doubt, always look to the real economy.

Our growing trade deficit, through 1987, without question, represented increasing amounts of business we were losing and represented slower economic growth than we would have had otherwise. The growing capital inflow was the financial mirror image of our lost business.

Thus, Mr. Thurow's comment that we are dependent on foreign funds is tantamount to saying that we are addicted to our trade deficit. We may have become accustomed to its presence, but to say that we're "hooked" on it is absurd. We're not *that* masochistic. If our current account deficit begins to shrink, so will the net capital inflow. And we will find that we are no more dependent on capital inflows than Germany and Japan are.

Foreigners have done us no favor in buying our securities. It has been to their benefit. They are more than happy to participate in our financial markets and to sell us goods for dollars. Sometimes they are so happy to do so that their governments subsidize their sales; or they sell their goods here at lower prices than at home.

But, some of you say, foreigners now hold large amounts of American securities. What if they suddenly decide to liquidate their holdings—dump them on the market all at once? Will that not precipitate a financial crisis? Given all the reasons that they elected to buy these securities in the first place—our healthy, large, open economy (even with slower growth); a safe haven for investment funds; and political uncertainties in other countries—I doubt very much that they would do that. Lower interest rates here might lead to some foreign selling of U.S. bonds. But declining interest rates mean a rising bond market. They would be selling into a strong market.

Besides, it is the Federal Reserve's job to maintain orderly markets. I am confident that they are fully capable of doing it, as they did after the October stock market debacles of 1987 and 1989. I think we have more to fear from Wall Street's program trading, insider trading, and the huge amounts of junk bonds outstanding than we do from investors in London, Frankfurt, Zurich, Tokyo, or anywhere else. If we are concerned about our financial markets, we would be better advised to pay more attention to Wall Street shenanigans.

Saying that foreigners will not want to hold dollars anymore means that they no longer would export goods to us and take payment in dollars. Would you believe that? On the contrary, I think that foreign governments and businesses want to support the dollar's foreign exchange value so they can remain competitive and continue to export to the United States.

There is a basic logical flaw in the hooked-on-foreign-investment arguments by Feldstein, Thurow, and others. In our national income, or GNP accounts, saving equals investment by definition at all times and at all levels. That fact does not tell you how you get to any particular level of equality.

When these economists say that if foreign investment here (the capital inflow) were to shrink, domestic investment would be correspondingly less, they are maintaining the definitional equality of saving and investment. What they do not tell you—and here is the flaw—is that they are taking as *given* total savings, total investment, household saving, corporate saving, government dis-saving (the budget deficit), and total business activity or GNP.

But if net foreign investment in the United States were to shrink, we could no longer take these things as given. A drop in net capital inflow means a smaller trade deficit (as I pointed out above), which means more business activity in the United States, which in turn means more household and corporate saving and less government dis-saving (because of increased budget revenue). Saving and investment would still be equal, but at a higher level. In the end, the increased business activity would raise business investment—not lower it—and the greater amount of investment would be financed domestically.

If you are still skeptical, you do not have to take only my word for it. Any respectable econometric model—say, University of Michigan, DRI, Wharton, or BEA (at the Commerce Department)—will produce precisely this result.

One caveat (if I may be permitted an assumption) is whether the Federal Reserve will accommodate the increase in business activity. They will, if inflation does not threaten to accelerate. What is *not* in question is that a decline in our current account deficit, together with the capital inflow, will *stimulate* business activity.

As with saving and investment, the equality of the current account balance and the net capital inflow does not tell us why they are at any particular level. Earlier, I offered four factors that underlay the rise in our foreign trade deficit. The process might have begun with any of them. Table 4–1 traces some of these developments during the past decade.

Of the two economic factors—relative economic growth and the dollar—it is clear that the dollar had the first impact on our trade deficit. It rose 41 percent from the end of 1980 to the end of 1984 against a group of 15 major currencies. Obviously, the dollar rose by varying amounts against each one. This index is a weighted average in which the weights applied to the 15 currencies are determined by the amounts of trade between the United States and the other individual countries.

TABLE 4–1
U.S. International Accounts and Their Effects on the Domestic Economy (Seasonally Adjusted, Annual Rate)

	1980	1981	1982	1983	1984	1985	1986	1987	1988	1989
Exchange value of the dollar (December value)[a]	92.0	100.3	111.3	118.0	129.5	116.1	102.5	87.4	86.2	89.7
Current account balance ($billion)	1.5	8.2	−7.0	−44.3	−104.2	−112.7	−133.2	−143.7	−126.5	−113.5[b]
Merchandise trade balance ($billion)	−25.5	−28.0	−36.4	−67.1	−122.5	−122.1	−145.1	−159.5	−127.2	−111.6[b]
Balance of receipts on income from assets ($billion)	30.4	34.1	28.7	24.9	18.5	25.9	21.6	22.3	2.2	−7.9[b]
Ratio of imports to final demand expenditure (1982 $)										
Capital goods except autos (%)	18.2	19.3	21.0	23.5	29.8	28.9	32.9	36.5	39.3	40.3
Motor vehicles (%)	24.8	25.0	26.2	27.3	28.6	29.5	33.0	36.3	34.3	33.7
Consumer durable goods except autos (%)	16.4	16.9	16.2	17.0	19.4	19.8	21.6	21.7	21.7	21.7
Consumer nondurable goods (%)	5.8	6.0	6.2	7.0	8.6	8.5	9.6	10.6	11.0	11.2
Net foreign investment (net inflow (−))	+13.0	+10.6	−1.0	−33.5	−90.9	−114.4	−135.8	−150.9	−117.5	−99.8
Growth in gross domestic purchases (1982 $, 4th Quarter/4th Quarter, %)	−1.1	0.9	−0.8	8.4	6.4	4.3	2.1	4.6	2.4	2.1
Growth in GNP (1982 $, 4th Quarter/4th Quarter, %)	−0.1	0.6	−1.9	6.5	5.1	3.6	1.9	5.4	3.4	2.4

[a]U.S. trade-weighted value of the dollar, 15 currencies (1980–82 = 100), Morgan Guaranty Bank.
[b]First three quarters 1989 at an annual rate.

Source: Bureau of Economic Analysis

The dollar actually began rising in the third quarter of 1980 and reached its peak in the first quarter of 1985. In all, our currency went up by about one half. Its rise reflected a shift by foreigners and Americans toward more investments in the United States for the reasons discussed earlier. Note that while foreign investors began to bid up the dollar in late 1980, the net inflow of capital (net foreign investment) did not begin until 1982, when our merchandise trade deficit was large enough to pull the current account balance into the red.

This shift was then reinforced after 1981 by the Latin American debt problems which cut down our exports and then after 1982 by our strong economic rebound which propelled imports upward. The surge in imports reflected, then, the effects of the strong dollar as well as the strong business expansion. The pace of the expansion moderated after 1984, but the high dollar carried the trade deficit to a peak in 1987. At that point, the net capital inflow (net foreign investment) also reached a peak of $151 billion. As business shifted abroad, economic growth slowed to a crawl in 1986, with GNP rising a puny 1.9 percent.

The effects of business shifting abroad, are evident in the rest of the table. Foreign producers captured a large part of U.S. domestic markets. For capital equipment, traditionally an American stronghold, their share has gone from 18 percent in 1980 to 40 percent in 1989. Foreign automakers enlarged their slice from 25 percent to 34 percent during the same period. It would have grown much more than that were it not for the "voluntary restraint agreements" (quotas). They also increased their share for a wide variety of consumer goods and for other products not shown in this table.

The result, in aggregate, was to slow the growth of GNP while the trade balance was sinking between 1981 and 1987. The last two lines of the table are instructive. "Gross domestic purchases" represents everything we buy. Gross national product (GNP) is everything we produce. In each year from 1981 through 1986, GNP grew less than our purchases did, as production was shifting abroad; and GNP grew less than it would have if the production had remained here.

With faster growth in GNP, unemployment would have declined faster, incomes would have grown faster, poverty would have shrunk faster, and individuals and businesses could have purchased more consumer and capital goods. The trade deficit and associated capital inflow—for which Feldstein, Thurow, and the Brookings authors are so grateful— have been, in fact, a heavy anchor restraining our economy.

The Deficit Reduction Act of 1984, drafted and legislated during Don Regan's watch at the Treasury Department, included a provision which repealed withholding taxes on interest paid to foreigners. It was not a particularly large revenue item, but it did encourage foreigners to buy more American securities. As a result, the dollar was pushed up further than it would have been otherwise. It rose 6 percent during 1983 and seemed to be slowing; however, it jumped nearly another 10 percent in 1984.

The provision was unnecessary, ill-conceived, ill-timed and harmful to our economy. Faced with high and rising currencies, other countries have taken effective measures to stem the tide. Switzerland once applied negative interest rates to foreign funds. In 1984, we would have been better advised to move in that direction than to encourage still more inflow.

Our policies not only caused nearly all of our producers to lose market share, it drove many of them out of business. Our consumer electronics industry was particularly devastated. We produce no VCRs in the United States, few television sets, and a limited amount of other products.

At the beginning of the decade, our international trade in autos and parts was in deficit by about $11 billion. The high-flying dollar helped introduce so many Americans to foreign cars that by 1987 the deficit was nearly $58 billion, with only a slight improvement in 1988. Despite the dollar's decline, I fear that the deficit for this sector will give way grudgingly at best. *Consumer Reports* indicates that imported cars are more reliable than American automobiles. And other surveys suggest that imported cars enjoy very high levels of customer loyalty. Competitive pricing alone, therefore, may not do the job, except with very large price cuts. Perhaps our foreign trade in autos will get a boost from Japanese models that are now assembled in the United States.

Some other sectors, I believe, are beginning to respond to the lower dollar. Our foreign trade in chemicals was in the black by about $11 billion in 1980 to 1981. The surplus was squeezed down to $8 billion in 1985, but began to recover quickly as the dollar fell. By 1988, it reached nearly $14 billion.

Capital equipment was hit harder, but also is starting to rebound. A $45 billion surplus in 1980 to 1981 almost disappeared by 1987, falling to $2.6 billion before turning up again to $10.6 billion in 1988. Further improvement is likely if the dollar does not rise any further, but may be slow in coming as imports of capital equipment are still very strong.

Among the major end-use categories—food, industrial supplies, oil, capital goods, autos, consumer goods, and "other"—imports of capital goods increased the most. In real volume, only capital equipment and oil imports increased in 1988. It would have been better to have produced that equipment at home, but at least these imports added to our real capital stock. Of the large increase in imports from 1982 to 1988, more than half was in capital goods and industrial supplies. Less than half was in consumer goods. Similar proportions apply to the level of imports in 1988.

Contrast these facts, however, with the following two assertions:

1. "And the longer we continue to borrow from abroad, for no other purpose but to pay for our *overconsumption* [emphasis added], the farther our living standards will have to fall."[8]
2. "Ultimately, foreigners will not continue . . . to finance our excess spending, especially when their funds are devoted not to investment in productive assets but to *consumption* [emphasis added]."[9]

I guess if you're going to misrepresent the situation, it doesn't matter if you misstate the facts.

---

[8] Benjamin M. Friedman, *Day of Reckoning* (New York: Random House, 1988), p. 38.

[9] R. Z. Lawrence, "The International Dimension," in Litan et al., *American Living Standards*, p. 28.

But not to worry—this matter of "borrowing from abroad" is largely semantics. We are not becoming a "debtor nation" in any sense in which we apply that term to Latin American countries. And, more important, our living standards will not fall for those reasons.

One general area that shows an encouraging foreign trade record is high technology. Conventional analyses of trade by high-tech industries indicate that the balance fell into deficit in the late 1980s. But these industries also produce some low-tech products. The Census Bureau has aggregated the data by products, as well as by industries, producing a much more meaningful and a more favorable result.[10]

Table 4–2 traces the paths of trade balances for 10 product categories from 1982 to 1988. In total, our foreign trade for these products remained in surplus throughout the period, hitting a low point of $16 billion in 1986 and rebounding to $28 billion in 1988. Obviously, much of this favorable performance was in aerospace (mainly commercial aircraft) where a $12 billion surplus in 1982 grew to $20 billion in 1988. But other areas also more than held their own. The notable exception is electronics, where the balance worsened from 1982 to 1988.

For all 10 categories, exports surged from $40 billion in 1982, or 18 percent of total merchandise exports, to $77 billion in 1988—nearly doubling and accounting for 24 percent of 1988's exports. Meanwhile, imports of high-tech products rose from $15 billion in 1982, 6 percent of the total, to $49 billion in 1988, or 11 percent of the total. These are hardly signs that we are becoming a backward nation. Of course, we should promote further progress in these areas, and we can with an improved, permanent R&D tax credit and improved investment incentives. High-technology products are not just important for foreign trade, they are critical for domestic development.

The patterns of trade by industries and products are reflected in trade patterns by countries. Given the records for

---

[10]Bureau of the Census, *Statistical Brief SB-2-89*, August 1989.

TABLE 4–2
Advanced Technology Trade Balance (Millions of Dollars)

Technology	1982	1983	1984	1985	1986	1987	1988
Biotechnology	107	130	111	66	-50	-44	-148
Life science	2,045	1,755	1,560	1,366	1,047	1,186	2,135
Opto-electronics	175	194	167	48	-489	-520	-582
Computers and telecommunications	6,985	5,699	6,144	6,253	569	1,579	3,401
Electronics	-1,733	-2,328	-4,235	-2,573	-2,551	-3,201	-4,178
Computer manufacturing	2,141	2,315	2,656	3,867	1,954	2,284	3,972
Material design	1,424	1,703	1,849	1,083	1,727	2,655	2,970
Aerospace	11,945	13,012	10,814	12,671	12,450	14,967	19,565
Weapons	75	133	82	151	238	165	80
Nuclear technology	1,554	1,408	1,560	1,457	1,449	1,202	1,043
	24,718	24,020	20,708	24,388	16,343	20,272	28,258

Source: Bureau of the Census

autos and electronics, it is not surprising that our deficit with Japan remains huge. In 1980, we imported $10 billion more from Japan than we exported to that country. In 1987, the deficit was $57 billion, over one third of our total deficit of $160 billion. And while our total deficit shrank $32 billion in 1988, the deficit with Japan declined only $4 billion to $53 billion, with very little further progress in 1989.

Our deficit with Western Europe grew as much as it did with Japan. In 1980, we had a surplus of $20 billion, which shifted to a deficit of $28 billion by 1987, a downdraft of $48 billion. The difference is that this shortfall recovered to a $16 billion deficit in 1988 and is still improving.

At the present time, Latin American debt problems are controlling our trade pattern with those countries. At the beginning of the 1980s, our trade with them was in surplus; the balance sank to a $12 billion deficit in 1987, recovering to an $8 billion deficit in 1988. But this balance will have to remain in deficit if they are to accumulate dollars to service their external debts. (Or they will have to maintain a bigger surplus with other industrial countries—in dollars—than any deficit they have with us.) Basically, we cannot get back to a large surplus with those countries and still have them pay down their debts.

One of the more interesting developments has been our trade with the Asian newly industrialized countries—the so-called NICs—Taiwan, Korea, Singapore, and Hong Kong. Overall, our trade with these four countries was in deficit by $3.5 billion in 1980. By 1987, the red ink was up to $35 billion, with Taiwan and Korea accounting for $27 billion of that total. We had some improvement to $29 billion in 1988, with the deficit for Taiwan and Korea easing to $22 billion.

Further progress against the $22 billion will be slow at best, not because these two countries have products which are unique or special, but because they maintain price advantages through artificially low exchange rates. Both claim special privileges because they are developing countries and because they are clients of the United States. I have little sympathy for that argument. The special relationships can be accommodated in other ways. Their exchange rates are not determined in the free markets; they keep them at artificially low levels, providing their producers with unfair price advantages in our markets. They also maintain high import barriers. It is time we put an end to both practices.

You might have heard that wage rates in Taiwan or Korea are $2 to $3 per hour, compared to $12 to $15 in comparable industries in the United States. This does not mean we cannot fairly compete with companies producing those products abroad. For one thing, our productivity levels are still much higher than theirs. But more importantly, their wage rates are a fraction of ours, on a dollar basis, because of the low values of their currencies. The small exchange rate increases that they have permitted in recent years amount to very little.

During the 1930s, when all the industrial countries were suffering from very high unemployment, they occasionally tried to gain a competitive advantage by devaluing their currencies. The practice came to be known as "exchange dumping," a term coined, I believe, by the economist Ragnar Nurkse. Today, we use the expression "dumping" to refer to the practice of selling an individual product abroad at a price below the domestic price. By exchange dumping, a country can sell all of its products below the costs of foreign producers. But since its selling prices abroad are not—or need not be—below domestic prices, it is not dumping, according to today's agreements.

In my view, exchange dumping is a more serious unfair practice than today's concept of dumping. It is tolerated by the major industrial countries because Korea and Taiwan are small. If these countries accounted for a large share of world trade and were cutting seriously into European and Japanese business, I assure you that they wouldn't get away with it.

Treasury Secretaries Regan, Baker, and Brady, during the Reagan years and the early part of the Bush administration, insisted that exchange rates and related policies were strictly their responsibility. So much so, that no one else in the executive branch—except, of course, the president—could even mention any currencies without Treasury and White House rebuke. (Shades of Jimmy Carter.)

Of course, it is virtually impossible to talk about our economy and our trade balance without mentioning the dollar. At one point, I was considering referring to it as our "pineapple." But in permitting exchange rate dumping to persist, these Treasury Secretaries have represented American businesses and workers very poorly.

Our difficulties with Japan are more subtle and more complicated. The basic problem is simple—a $50 billion deficit that is receding painfully slowly. Not that we need have, or should even aim for, balance with each country or region; but we should aim for *global* balance. However, this will be impossible if we do not reduce our deficits substantially with Japan and the NICs.

But getting there will not be half the fun. U.S. imports from Japan are running close to $95 billion a year, about 20 percent of our total imports, and virtually all in manufactured goods. About one fourth of these Japanese goods are autos; the rest are divided among a wide variety of industrial and consumer products.

About 60 percent of our $45 billion in exports to Japan are manufactured goods. The rest are mainly lumber and lumber products and agricultural items. These exports have begun to grow more rapidly, as Japanese officials are quick to point out. But note that with exports only half of imports, they will have to grow well over twice as fast as imports to make any noticeable dent in the imbalance.

And achieving that dent means fighting our way through a variety of problems. Japanese officials acknowledge that their manufacturers have close, long-standing relationships with suppliers ("old boy networks," as we call them here), which our producers have had great difficulty breaking into.

Their internal distribution systems for consumer goods are ponderous and complex, with the result that prices are marked up enormously before the goods reach consumers. In the fall of 1989, a team of U.S. and Japanese government officials surveyed consumer prices in the two countries. At a time when the dollar was trading at about 142 yen, they found that 84 of the 122 products included were more expensive in Japan. Prices of 40 products were more than 50 percent higher. The only prices that were less in Japan were for electronic products, which are not imported from the United States in any meaningful quantity.[11] The system has the effect of holding down consumption relative to investment and makes it extremely difficult for our manufacturers to market their products there.

Only recently, after intensive complaints by industry and government officials, have they opened up some construction projects to foreign bidding in which our companies may compete. But it is still a small amount. They also maintain tight import quotas for our agricultural products in order to cater to a small, politically strong agricultural lobby.

I do not believe that we have the right to tell them how to organize and operate their economy, but we do have the right to participate in it through fair competition. However, they have systematically excluded outsiders (not just the United States) from doing that. In our negotiations with them, they are quick to divert attention to our budget deficit, which is none of their business, and our own quotas, which are. Typically, after several rounds of high-level negotiations, a new administration is in office in Washington, and we start all over again.

Akio Morita, Chairman of the Sony Corporation claims that one reason American companies are not competitive enough is their "short-term orientation" which "encourages the neglect of long-term investment vital to industry, depriving it of the ability to create attractive products. . . . Patience, consistency, and continuity are required."[12] With regard to U.S. business planning, he's right. We reward performance not by years, but by quarters.

I suspect that this "long-term orientation" also underlies their view of reducing the trade imbalance between our two countries. If our representatives continue to meet with them annually, or even semi-annually, to discuss our views and

---

[11]Price Comparisons May Cost Japanese . . . , *The Wall Street Journal*, November 8, 1989.

[12]Business: Trading with Japan, *New York Times*, October 1, 1989, Section 3, p. 1.

mutual interests, we may be looking at a 10- or 20-year process. What we need is something like what we used to call the "Chinese water torture"—a constant, almost daily prodding to fix, change, and open their markets step-by-step to fair competition. We would make far more progress with thousands of small steps than by aiming for a few giant ones.

I think it was John Maynard Keynes who once suggested that countries that run chronic balance-of-payments surpluses should be required to give them away. We ought to press for adoption of such a measure during the current GATT negotiations. It could be a way of reducing the imbalances and easing the LDC debt problems at the same time.

This would apply to all countries, not only to Japan. In 1988, for example, Germany's current account surplus amounted to about 4 percent of its GDP, Japan's about 3 percent. Germany, however, may need some of these resources to defray the costs of absorbing their brethren from the East.

Both the Europeans and the Japanese have pointed to our import barriers when we complain of theirs. And we do have them. In July 1989, the Bush administration announced a 30-month extension of import quotas for steel products. The industry had sought the same five-year extension it had been granted by President Reagan. During these two and a half years, our government negotiators will try to end foreign subsidies for their steel producers.

But this is not the main problem in the U.S. steel industry. Our steel producers cannot compete—even without foreign subsidies—because our industry wage rates are higher than theirs (and higher than average manufacturing wages in the United States). Meanwhile, productivity is below that of foreign producers. What we need is complete modernization of our industry.

Modernization will require a huge investment in new facilities. To remain competitive, the industry must engage in extensive, ongoing R & D of products and processes. We must remove *now* the fiscal impediments of high tax rates on equipment and little support for R & D. Otherwise, there is no point in throwing the industry into the competitive pool only to sink. After all, they're not the enemy, they're *us*.

If we will not provide the competitive backing—tax credits for investment and R & D—we should keep the quotas. This also applies to other industries which are under competitive siege and are under-armed. Quotas should be retained in any case for supplies from countries that maintain artificially low exchange rates.

Nonetheless, the proof of the pudding is in the results. At its peak, our trade deficit reached 4 percent of GNP, a level not one European country or Japan would have tolerated. Despite this deficit, our approach to trade problems has been to lower barriers around the world and expand trade; and we should continue our efforts in this direction.

The dollar's decline since early 1985 has put us in a more advantageous position. Labor Department data show that U.S. labor compensation costs are generally competitive at these exchange rates and, against the European economies, *strongly* competitive.[13] In 1988, European compensation in dollars was 5 percent higher than ours, Japan's 9 percent less. But in both cases, it is generally agreed that the level of our productivity is still higher than theirs. Because of this, we are moving toward trade balance with Europe and are probably on our way to regaining a surplus.

In the case of Japan, moving toward better balance in a reasonable time (not decades) probably will require a substantial increase in the value of the yen. I suspect, however, that they are encouraging their investors to maintain a strong, steady flow of investment funds toward the United States in order to hold the dollar up and thereby help their exporters.

I have spoken positively of the prospects for and efforts to reduce our trade deficit and hopefully move it back into surplus. Surely, those of you in manufacturing businesses and in internationally traded services would welcome a surge in foreign orders—and so would your employees. Do you know that some economists claim we would be worse off if our exports boomed, and we gained a trade surplus? Who could

---

[13]U.S. Department of Labor, Bureau of Labor Statistics, *International Comparisons of Hourly Compensation Costs,* Report 771, August 1989.

say that? No, not George Orwell practicing his "Newspeak" for *1984*. Naturally, it would be the same ones who tell you that you were better off when you lost all that business to foreign producers because then we had a "capital inflow"—the Boston-Brookings Axis.

You cannot believe they said that? Well, I did cite two references earlier in this chapter—Friedman and Lawrence— which warn of a lower standard of living awaiting you. Or, how about these comments? Lawrence observes that with our services accounts moving into deficit, we *"will have to run a trade surplus"* [emphasis added], to bring our current account into balance. "Domestic spending will thus have to fall below domestic production. To bring spending into line with production, the U.S. economy will have to engage in considerable belt tightening. . . . All told, U.S. living standards will be reduced. . . ."[14]

Does it frighten you that "we will *have to* run a trade surplus?" I thought that is something you would *want,* because it would mean more business for you.

We can achieve a trade surplus through an export boom and by recapturing part of our domestic markets. Surely you would welcome that. In that case, we do not have to accept the ominous view of his comment: "Domestic spending will thus have to *fall below* domestic production." How about taking the view that production and incomes can then rise above domestic spending?

It is not a matter of the glass is half empty versus the glass is half full. Lawrence and Friedman argue that U.S. consumption must fall and that if production rises above U.S. consumption it's bad. That is because, again, they take *as given* total output or growth in output—if exports rise, then consumption must fall.

But as production moves back onshore, it will add to economic growth. Lawrence acknowledges this at one point: "Since most trade occurs in goods, the projections [trade balance or surplus] *imply a major expansion in the manufac-*

---

[14]Litan et al., *American Living Standards,* pp. 37–38.

turing sector." And he acknowledges also that we have the industrial capacity to accommodate this expansion.[15] But these acknowledgements did not affect his basic approach or conclusions.

The truth is that you were hurt when you lost business to foreigners, and you will benefit as the business comes back. The reason that more interest and dividends will be paid to foreigners is that they raised their incomes and savings here through their trade surplus with us. *We have already taken the hit.* If the trade deficit shrinks, and our foreign trade moves into surplus, it will *add* to our incomes and wealth. You can then make up your own minds whether you are better or worse off.

The interest and dividends paid to foreigners will be a small share of our growing output and will be accommodated by it. Yes, the old wounds will continue to ooze some income payments. They already own the assets. But what you earn in wages and salaries from your own labors and in interest and dividends from your financial assets *will be yours to keep!* If the Brookings-Boston axis keeps on telling you that your standard of living is falling, while your business activity and your wealth are rising, ignore them. President Reagan came close to abolishing the Council of Economic Advisers because of advice like that.

But our opponents, the Brookings-Boston crowd, believe they represent most mainstream professional thinking, and they may still come back at us, "You admit, Ortner, that 'we have already taken the hit', as you succinctly put it. But it was a 'big hit,' so to speak, and we piled up a mountain of debt from all those trade deficits. Now, we make Mexico, Brazil, Argentina, et al., look like pikers, because we are the world's largest debtor."

Or are we?

---

[15]Ibid., pp. 45–46.

Chapter Five

"THE 'JAPS' ARE COMING, THE 'JAPS' ARE COMING"

Myths: 1. The United States is now the world's largest debtor, larger than all of Latin America combined. 2. Foreigners are buying up America and are beginning to run our country.

Facts: 1. The United States doesn't have debts like the Latin Americans'! 2. If foreigners have assets in the United States, just who controls whom? Besides, it's peanuts.

International investment, like international trade, is beneficial to the world's economy and to the countries, businesses, and individuals who participate in it. The theory is simple: Capital moves toward those countries, regions, or industries that offer the greatest returns. To the extent that this is true, the process maximizes aggregate output and incomes. Therefore, it should not only be tolerated, but encouraged by all countries. And the benefits are not just economic. International investment generally promotes good political and social relationships among countries. At least it has the potential to do so and does, I believe, most of the time. Isolation is damaging.

But, as in foreign trade, the real world does not always conform to the ideal model. Given the practical complexities of real-world risks and uncertainties, *maximizing returns* can mean anything from short-term, quick, speculative profits to long-term survival.

Within these extreme considerations lies a broad range of economic and financial incentives, some of which I referred to earlier: participating in an attractive and promising market, production facilities in a low-labor-cost country, the often-quoted safe haven for funds, financial investment for higher interest rates and rising equity prices, diversifying to protect against fluctuating exchange rates, and establishing production facilities behind the iron curtains of protective trade barriers. (Now that these curtains are crumbling across Europe, we should keep Churchill's marvelous metaphor alive in some other application.) I am sure these few suggestions raise many others in your minds.

The process is not as simple, therefore, as maximizing returns. But that does not mean we should discard the fundamental premise of encouraging international investment, even though several of these incentives converged during the 1980s to produce an excessive "inflow" to our detriment. In this, as in other endeavors, it is possible to overdo a good thing. For the United States, there have been costs as well as benefits. While the distinctions among types of investment are somewhat blurred, I would still maintain that foreign direct investment in U.S. productive facilities has been beneficial on balance. The excess has come in the form of financial investment and speculation, which drove up the exchange value of the dollar.

In observing earlier that the net inflow of capital is equal to our current account deficit, I did not mean or imply that international investment depends on trade imbalances. Causality can run in either direction, from investment flows to trade imbalances or vice versa. For the United States in the 1980s, large-scale foreign investment here was one of the main causes of our trade deficit.

But investment can proceed, also, in large volumes, in an environment of balanced world trade. That would mean that foreign investment here and our investment abroad would be of similar magnitudes. Our policy should be to accommodate a capital inflow, especially into real investment, just as we ask foreign countries to accept our investments, consistent with a reasonable balance in our merchandise trade.

In 1985, net foreign investment in the United States (the GNP version of the current account deficit) reached $114 billion, heading toward a peak of $151 billion in 1987. Foreigners accumulated assets here, net of U.S. acquisitions abroad, in roughly these amounts. The equality between our current account deficit and net foreign accumulation of assets here is necessarily true. As our favorite textbook authors, Samuelson and Nordhaus, explain: "The United States must have either borrowed or run down its assets. For it is definitional that what you buy you must either pay for or owe for."[1] (For some reason, this comment reminds me of an old Wall Street couplet for short selling: "He who sells what isn't his'n, Must buy it back or go to prison.")

Note that our authors acknowledge two means of settling the current account deficit—borrowing or paying (which is the same thing as running down your assets.) But then they present a summary of the United States balance of payments in 1987 and state that we settled the current account deficit strictly by borrowing abroad. In their words, "in 1987 the United States was a net *borrower* [emphasis theirs]: we were doing more borrowing abroad than foreigners were doing here."[2] Thus, they claim that we did not pay for our imports, we only owe for them.

This seems also to be the general view of the press. Ever since 1985, newspaper stories and editorials have uniformly trumpeted dire warnings about U.S. foreign debts. A typical example: **America's Role As Net Debtor**

> Last week the Commerce Department released what seems like an alarming statistic: The nation's *foreign debt* [emphasis added] more than doubled last year (1986), to $263 billion— well above the foreign debt of Brazil, Mexico, and Argentina combined. Furthermore, by 1992 the American debt will have risen to $900 billion, many economists estimate.[3]

---

[1]Paul Samuelson and William D. Nordhaus, *Economics,* 13th ed. (New York: McGraw-Hill, 1989), p. 912.

[2]Ibid., p. 913.

[3]Economic Scene, *New York Times,* July 1, 1987, p. D2.

Actually, there is *less* to this story than meets the eye, and less to worry about than the press claims. (Of course, that's nearly always true, no matter what the press writes about). This characterization of the United States position troubles many economists and especially many business people who thought they had *paid* for the goods and services they imported. Yet we also seem to *owe* for the imports. Surely it can't be true that we both paid and owe.

The problem is partly semantic—or definitional. Our economy operates mainly on credit (or "debt"). Bank deposits, which we individuals think of as our assets, are liabilities of the banks. When we import goods and *pay* for them by writing a check, the foreign exporter then owns the deposit. The bank's liability is then to a foreigner and, suddenly, we have become a debtor nation. Technically and literally, we are a debtor, even though we paid for the goods.

But if the foreigner then buys a hotel or builds a factory here, or simply buys United States common stocks with that deposit, we would, also literally, no longer be a debtor nation. Nonetheless, Samuelson and The New York Times would still call us a foreign debtor. Both incorrectly regard all foreign assets here as debt even though a large portion is in equities, direct investment, and real estate.

The Commerce Department, through the Bureau of Economic Analysis (BEA), did release those numbers, but did not label the United States a debtor nation. The BEA report is an annual release entitled *U.S. Net International Investment Position,* a more accurate description. And the figure in question has since been revised to $268 billion. But that's not important. The report shows foreign direct investment in the United States and U.S. direct investment abroad, U.S. and foreign purchases of securities, and large amounts of bank borrowing and lending to finance daily business activity and investment here and abroad. But it shows no U.S. government borrowing of foreign currencies to finance either our imports or our budget deficits.

The comparison of the U.S. international investment position with Latin American debt has, in fact, become commonplace. Many writers have pointed out "disquieting similarities."[4] Not only is this assessment incorrect, it could be dangerous if our policymakers ever came to believe it. They might conclude that our economic profligacy required substantial belt tightening. Thus, we could be pushed into the impoverishment of economic recession to avoid the impoverishment of phantom foreign indebtedness. Rather, we should be working harder to improve our competitive performance.

In truth, an objective comparison of our international position with that of the Latin American countries finds many more "quieting dissimilarities." It is something like daytime and nighttime; they are similar in that they are both parts of the day; and at the vernal and autumnal equinoxes, they are equal in length. At those times, you might even find some economists arguing that one causes the other (which, as usual, would not explain much) or that they are the same thing. For practical purposes, they're not. They are as different as, well, night and day.

Among the quieting dissimilarities between the United States and LDC foreign debt, I cite the following: First, the LDCs need foreign goods—equipment and consumer products—for their subsistence as well as development. They cannot produce it themselves. They also don't have the money to pay, so they borrow abroad in foreign currencies. We don't have to do either. We could produce most of these goods and finance our activity ourselves.

Second, foreigners choose to invest here. They drive up the dollar and thereby capture our markets (here and abroad) with their "cheapened" goods. Thus, we have not and need not go to foreigners with hat in hand. The process is detrimental to us.

Third, our government does not have obligations abroad in foreign currencies. The United States Treasury has no scheduled payments due to foreigners apart from its domestic

---

[4]I believe this expression was used by William McChesney Martin, Chairman of the Federal Reserve Board, in comparing the economy in the early 1960s with its state in 1929.

refunding schedules. Foreigners who purchase our Treasury's securities are simply participating in our market. After all, it's a free country; and they may also leave when they please. We don't need them.

The debt problem for the developing countries began with the first oil embargo and price hikes of 1973 to 1974. The jump in oil prices produced huge trade deficits for these countries, and—rather than reduce other imports and lower their already meager living standards (because they could not pay)— they began actively borrowing in the world's financial markets. Despite its position as an oil exporter, Mexico also borrowed heavily to finance development of its nationalized oil industry and imports of other goods that were rising rapidly in price.

A large part of the LDC debt problem derives from the fact that these countries did not borrow their own currencies, *they borrowed dollars.* By the end of 1988, Mexico owed $107 billion; Brazil, $120 billion; and Argentina, $60 billion.[5] Most of these borrowings are guaranteed by, and therefore are obligations of, the respective governments. Somewhat more than half of the debt is owed to banks, mainly American; the rest is long-term borrowing. Obviously, the short-term bank loans are the immediate concern, but the debt structure is not the problem.

The problem is the size of the debt, in dollars, in relation to their economies. In Mexico's case, the debt amounts to over three quarters of its GDP, the others somewhat less. To service the debts, these countries must earn surplus dollars through exports; and in that, they are badly strapped. Interest alone amounts to about one third of their total exports of goods and services. In recent years, their trade surpluses have not been large enough to cover service costs.

But it is not just interest costs. More seriously, their currencies are falling relative to the dollar. Relative to the peso, the dollar more than doubled in 1987. Therefore, so did Mexico's debt as measured in pesos. In 1988, the dollar rose

---

[5]World Bank, *World Debt Tables, 1988–1989.*

by two thirds against the peso, and by another 15 percent or so in 1989. From their perspective, paying in dollars has meant effectively having to say they are sorry.

Even by the early 1980s, it had become clear that Mexico's debt problem was unmanageable. During the 1981 to 1982 worldwide recession, demand for LDC exports was soft. And when oil prices and our oil imports weakened, Mexico announced that it could not continue to meet its foreign obligations. The other countries were clearly in the same predicament.

Solutions that satisfy both lenders and borrowers have been elusive. And for the rest of the decade, we saw a succession of proposals that did not work. A study by the International Monetary Fund suggested that one development that could have alleviated this debt burden was faster growth in the industrial countries. That would have lifted LDC exports. But faster growth, other than in the United States, was not forthcoming.

Finally, in July 1989, the Finance Minister of Mexico informed the U.S. Treasury Department that some accommodation would have to be made, or Mexico might take unilateral action. Secretary Brady reportedly contacted the American banks, which had been dragging their feet in the hope of a taxpayer bailout, to inform them that the bailout was not coming and that an agreement must be reached. Within three days, they had a "done deal" (as they say in Washington), involving some combination of debt reduction, lower interest rates, and/or new loans.[6] It remains to be seen, of course, whether the changes will be sufficient for Mexico to get on with its economic development as well as meet its reduced obligations.

A massive public bailout of the banks' bad loans would have been outrageous. The banks are writing down these bad loans, finally acknowledging their poor business judgment. Their error, apparently, was in violating the first rule of banking: "Never lend money to anyone unless he doesn't need it."

---

[6]How the Mexican Debt Pact Was Achieved, *New York Times,* July 31, 1989, p. D1.

The entire process was described prophetically several years ago by editors of *The Economist* in their usual clever fashion: *"International loans* may be: *development loans,* to countries that do not intend to pay them back; *loans on IMF conditions,* to countries forced to stage a slump before they get them; *nonperforming loans,* to help pay interest on previous loans that the recipients could not afford. A *banking crash* occurs when banks stop paying themselves the interest on their nonperforming loans."[7]

The U.S. government has no need to borrow abroad. Therefore, foreign investors—as well as bankers—are anxious to lend it money. Foreigners are able to do this by purchasing securities in the open market. And they seem to be delighted to participate in our economy.

The mindless and endless parallels drawn between the U.S. position and that of the Latin American countries prompted Milton Friedman (remember, he's the *right* Friedman) to observe: "It is a mystery to me why, to take a specific example, it is regarded as a sign of Japanese strength and U.S. weakness that the Japanese find it more attractive to invest in the U.S. than in Japan. Surely it is the reverse—a sign of U.S. strength and Japanese weakness."[8]

Well, I would not go quite so far as to refer to it as "Japanese weakness." After all, they do invest intensively at home, also. But the important point is that their heavy investment here does not represent foreign aid to us—Friedman's right. And I might add that Europeans have even more assets here than the Japanese do. What about American firms? If they invest more here and less abroad, does that signify relative U.S. weakness? A number of writers have gone so far as to suggest that, in view of our "net debtor" position, the United States has lapsed again into the status of a developing nation. I hope so. "Developing" is all right; "underdeveloped" would be regrettable.

---

[7]Glossary 1983, *The Economist,* January 8, 1983, p. 4.

[8]Why the Twin Deficits Are a Blessing, *The Wall Street Journal,* December 14, 1988, Op-Ed page.

Table 5–1 shows the U.S. International Investment Position.[9] The data represent year-end values for each year 1973 through 1988. They correspond to a business firm's balance sheet in that they represent total amounts of ownership at a point in time. The BEA quarterly reports of U.S. international transactions correspond to a business firm's income statements. The transactions statements show balances on trade, goods and services, and current account, as well as inflows and outflows of capital. The accumulation of capital flows in the transactions statements correspond to year-to-year changes in the international investment position (*IIP*), similar to the relationship between income statements and balance sheets.

As the data indicate, at year-end 1985, foreigners owned slightly more than $1 trillion in assets in the United States, compared with U.S. ownership of about $950 billion in assets abroad. Thus, our international investment position was a negative $111 billion. The position declined steadily to negative $533 billion at the end of 1988 and will continue to decline faster or slower, depending on the size of our current account deficit, until the current account is brought into balance. At that point, the investment position will stabilize. It will increase, or would increase, year by year, approximately in the amount of any U.S. current account surpluses.

At the end of 1988, foreigners owned nearly $1.8 trillion in assets here. About $332 billion were held by official institutions, mainly in the form of U.S. Treasury securities. The rest, $1.5 trillion, were privately owned. Of this amount, about one third was in treasury and corporate securities. Combined official and private holdings of U.S. treasuries, $347 billion, amounted to slightly more than 15 percent of the $2.2 trillion in federal government debt outstanding. Certainly, that does not support the claim that foreigners have financed all of our budget deficits.

The largest single item is liabilities of U.S. banks, $609 billion in deposits and borrowings. On the other side of the ledger, U.S. banks had $603 billion in assets abroad. A

---

[9]Bureau of Economic Analysis, *Survey of Current Business* (Washington, D.C.: U.S. Department of Commerce, June 1989), p. 43.

TABLE 5–1

International Investment Position of the United States at Yearend, 1973–88 (Millions of Dollars)

Line	Type of investment	1973	1974	1975	1976	1977	1978
1	Net international investment position of the United States (line 2 less line 20).	47,894	58,731	74,240	83,578	72,741	76,115
2	U.S. assets abroad	222,430	255,719	295,100	347,160	379,105	447,847
3	U.S. official reserve assets. . .	14,378	15,883	16,226	18,747	19,314	18,650
4	Gold	11,652	11,652	11,599	11,598	11,719	11,671
5	Special drawing rights	2,166	2,374	2,335	2,395	2,629	1,558
6	Reserve position in the International Monetary Fund	552	1,852	2,212	4,434	4,946	1,047
7	Foreign currencies	8	5	80	321	20	4,374
8	U.S. Government assets, other than official reserve assets	38,807	38,331	41,804	45,994	49,544	54,200
9	U.S. loans and other long-term assets	36,187	36,268	39,809	44,124	47,749	52,252
10	Repayable in dollars	30,617	33,030	36,815	41,309	45,154	49,817
11	Other	5,570	3,238	2,994	2,815	2,595	2,435
12	U.S. foreign currency holdings and U.S. short-term assets	2,620	2,063	1,995	1,870	1,795	1,948
13	U.S. private assets	169,245	201,505	237,070	282,418	310,247	374,997
14	Direct investment abroad . .	101,313	110,078	124,050	136,809	145,990	162,727
15	Foreign securities	27,446	28,203	34,913	44,157	49,439	53,384
16	Bonds	17,420	19,192	25,328	34,704	39,329	42,148
17	Corporate stocks.	10,026	9,011	9,585	9,453	10,110	11,236
18	U.S. claims on unaffiliated foreigners reported by U.S. nonbanking concerns.	13,767	16,989	18,340	20,317	22,256	28,070
19	U.S. claims reported by U.S. banks, not included elsewhere.	26,719	46,235	59,767	81,135	92,562	130,816

Source: Bureau of Economic Analysis, *Survey of Current Business*, June 1989, p. 43.

1979	1980	1981	1982	1983	1984	1985	1986	1987	1988
94,457	106,260	140,916	136,703	89,004	3,300	−111,437	−267,803	−378,300	−532,534
510,563	607,090	719,612	824,755	873,457	895,853	949,667	1,073,344	1,169,679	1,253,671
18,956	26,756	30,075	33,957	33,748	34,933	43,185	48,510	45,797	47,802
11,172	11,160	11,151	11,148	11,121	11,096	11,090	11,064	11,078	11,057
2,724	2,610	4,096	5,250	5,025	5,641	7,293	8,395	10,283	9,637
1,253	2,852	5,054	7,348	11,312	11,541	11,947	11,730	11,349	9,745
3,807	10,134	9,774	10,212	6,289	6,656	12,856	17,322	13,086	17,363
58,423	63,768	68,677	74,584	79,491	84,836	87,620	89,543	88,513	85,484
56,477	62,023	67,201	72,884	77,814	82,883	85,817	88,759	87,638	84,880
54,085	59,799	64,959	70,948	75,991	81,103	84,090	87,161	86,024	83,403
2,392	2,224	2,242	1,936	1,823	1,780	1,727	1,598	1,614	1,477
1,946	1,745	1,476	1,700	1,677	1,953	1,803	784	875	604
433,184	516,566	620,860	716,213	760,218	776,084	818,862	935,291	1,035,369	1,120,385
187,858	215,375	228,348	207,752	207,203	211,480	230,250	259,800	307,983	326,900
56,800	62,653	63,151	75,300	83,393	88,917	112,226	131,736	146,713	156,758
41,966	43,487	45,791	56,732	57,529	61,900	72,934	81,723	92,044	94,027
14,834	19,166	17,360	18,568	25,864	27,017	39,292	50,013	54,669	62,731
31,497	34,672	35,853	28,583	35,117	30,056	29,023	36,417	31,216	32,900
157,029	203,866	293,508	404,578	434,505	445,631	447,363	507,338	549,457	603,828

TABLE 5–1 (*Concluded*)

Line	Type of investment	1973	1974	1975	1976	1977	1978
20	Foreign assets in the United States.................	174,536	196,988	220,860	263,582	306,364	371,730
21	Foreign official assets in the United States	69,266	79,865	86,910	104,445	140,867	173,057
22	U.S. Government securities............	53,777	58,072	63,553	72,572	105,386	128,511
23	U.S. Treasury securities .	52,903	56,504	61,107	70,555	101,092	123,991
24	Other...............	874	1,568	2,446	2,017	4,294	4,520
25	Other U.S. Government liabilities	2,388	2,726	4,215	8,860	10,260	12,749
26	U.S. liabilities reported by U.S. banks, not included elsewhere.	12,595	18,420	16,262	17,231	18,004	23,327
27	Other foreign official assets	506	647	2,880	5,782	7,217	8,470
28	Other foreign assets in the United States	105,270	117,123	133,950	159,137	165,497	198,673
29	Direct investment in the United States	20,556	25,144	27,662	30,770	34,595	42,471
30	U.S. Treasury securities ...	958	1,655	4,245	7,028	7,562	8,910
31	U.S. securities other than U.S. Treasury securities .	46,116	34,892	45,663	54,913	51,235	53,554
32	Corporate and other bonds	12,600	10,671	10,025	11,964	11,456	11,457
33	Corporate stocks.......	33,516	24,221	35,638	42,949	39,779	42,097
34	U.S. liabilities to unaffiliated foreigners reported by U.S. nonbanking concerns.	11,712	13,586	13,905	12,961	11,921	16,019
35	U.S. liabilities reported by U.S. banks, not included elsewhere.	25,928	41,846	42,475	53,465	60,184	77,719

1979	1980	1981	1982	1983	1984	1985	1986	1987	1988
416,106	500,830	578,696	688,052	784,453	892,553	1,061,104	1,341,147	1,547,979	1,786,205
159,852	176,062	180,425	189,109	194,468	199,300	202,745	241,947	283,552	322,103
106,640	118,189	125,130	132,587	136,987	143,014	143,440	177,283	218,929	259,249
101,748	111,336	117,004	124,929	129,716	135,510	135,740	170,596	211,078	250,287
4,892	6,853	8,126	7,658	7,271	7,504	7,700	6,687	7,851	8,962
12,749	13,367	13,029	13,639	14,231	14,971	15,850	17,991	15,471	14,187
30,540	30,381	26,737	24,989	25,534	26,090	26,734	27,920	31,838	31,507
9,923	14,125	15,529	17,894	17,716	15,225	16,721	18,753	17,314	17,160
256,254	324,768	398,271	498,943	589,985	693,253	858,359	1,099,200	1,264,427	1,464,103
54,462	83,046	108,714	124,677	137,061	164,583	184,615	220,414	271,788	328,851
14,210	16,113	18,505	25,758	33,846	58,195	83,636	91,498	78,339	96,626
58,587	74,114	75,085	92,988	113,811	127,272	206,153	308,773	344,257	393,623
10,269	9,545	10,694	16,709	17,454	32,724	82,479	142,120	170,831	195,186
48,318	64,569	64,391	76,279	96,357	94,548	123,674	166,653	173,426	198,437
18,669	30,426	30,606	27,532	26,937	31,024	29,458	26,902	29,404	35,532
110,326	121,069	165,361	227,988	278,330	312,179	354,497	451,613	540,639	609,471

large part of these totals reflects the fact that the dollar is an international currency, used in payments among other countries. U.S. banks have many overseas offices that participate in and finance these operations. Almost half of the U.S. banks' liabilities of $609 billion was owed to their own foreign offices, while claims on their own foreign offices similarly amounted to about 42 percent of the $603 billion in total bank claims.

Both assets and liabilities contain some foreign currency denominations, but these are essentially to facilitate client operations and not generally long-term commitments. Changes in bank claims and liabilities also reflect interest rate differentials among the world's financial centers, and adjustments to take advantage of lower financing costs and higher investment yields.

Also worth noting are U.S. direct investment abroad and foreign direct investment in the United States. *Direct investment* is defined for this purpose as a 10 percent or larger ownership interest in a business enterprise. Of all the different avenues of international investment, this comes closest to real investment—equipment and bricks and mortar. However, it also involves pure equity transactions and takeovers. You will not be surprised, therefore, if I argue that this is the most beneficial form of international investment, especially to the country that is host to the inflow. It is the purely speculative, or "hot money," that we could have done without. It is also the "hot money" that may take flight someday and temporarily disrupt our financial markets. At the end of 1988, foreigners owned close to $330 billion in direct investments in the United States, about 18 percent of their total assets here; by coincidence, the total was just about the same as our reported direct investment position abroad. For the U.S. side, direct investment amounted to slightly more than one quarter of total foreign assets.

Table 5–2 (on page 124) shows how the BEA measures the changes in investment values and the year-end positions for 1987 and 1988, by types of assets and by world positions.[10]

---

[10]Ibid., p. 42.

Changes in asset values consist of four components: new capital flows, which are generally the largest part; price changes; changes in value because of exchange rate movements; and miscellaneous adjustments. *Price changes* refers to financial market values; these are applied so that changes in bond and stock market levels are included in year-end valuations, both for our holdings abroad and foreign holdings here.

Adjustments for exchange rate movements were generally small and applied more to our assets abroad than to our liabilities. The adjustment for foreign assets in the United States was small in 1988 because the dollar changed little—rising a few percentage points on balance—but mainly because only a very small part of our liabilities are denominated in foreign currencies. The entire adjustment, minus $1,967 million, was reflected in corporate and other bonds. When the dollar rose, the liabilities in foreign currencies were worth less.

Similarly, our assets abroad, which were in foreign currencies, also were worth less, resulting in a markdown of $7,863 million. In 1987, when the dollar fell about 15 percent on average (the other currencies rose relative to the dollar), our liabilities were marked up $5,798 million and our assets raised $21,083 million, a net gain of over $15 billion.

The investment positions by geographical regions are equally, if not more, interesting. You have been hearing a great deal in recent years about how the Japanese are "buying up" or "taking over" America. At the end of 1988, they owned $285 billion worth of assets here. At the same time, Western European interests owned $868 billion worth, three times as much. Individuals and businesses in Latin America and other Western hemisphere countries, apart from Canada, held $327 billion in assets here.

Of the $1,254 billion in U.S. assets abroad, $431 billion, or one third, were in Western Europe; $303 billion, or about one fourth, were in Latin America and Other Western hemisphere countries. In 1988, we still had a positive investment balance with Canada, $155 billion there versus $101 billion here. However, our population is nearly 10 times as large as theirs. On a per capita basis, they own six times as many assets here as we do there.

TABLE 5-2

International Investment Position of the United States at Yearend, 1987 and 1988 [Millions of Dollars]

Line	Type of Investment	Position 1987	Changes in Position in 1988 (Decrease (−))					Position 1988
			Attributable to:				Total (a+b+ c+d)	
				Valuation Adjustments				
			Capital Flows (a)	Price Changes (b)	Ex- change Rate Changes (c)	Other Changes (d)		
1	Net international investment position of the United States (line 2 less line 20).	−378,300	−137,189	−14,190	−5,900	3,041	−154,234	−532,534
2	U.S. assets abroad	1,169,679	82,110	8,507	−7,863	1,238	83,992	1,253,671
3	U.S. official reserve assets.	45,797	3,566	. . .	−1,539	−21	2,005	47,802
4	Gold	11,078	. . .	. . .	. . .	−21	−21	11,057
5	Special drawing rights.	10,283	−474	. . .	−173	. . .	−646	9,637
6	Reserve position in the International Monetary Fund.	11,349	−1,025	. . .	−580	. . .	−1,604	9,745
7	Foreign currencies .	13,086	5,064	. . .	−787	. . .	4,277	17,363
8	U.S. Government assets, other than off. res. assets.	88,513	−2,999	. . .	−16	−15	−3,029	85,484
9	U.S. loans and other long-term assets	87,638	−2,733	. . .	−11	−14	−2,758	84,880
10	Repayable in dollars.	86,024	−2,667	. . .	. . .	45	−2,621	83,403
11	Other.	1,614	−67	. . .	−11	−59	−137	1,477
12	U.S. foreign currency holdings and U.S. short- term assets.	875	−265	. . .	−5	−1	−271	604
13	U.S. private assets. . .	1,035,369	81,543	8,507	−6,308	1,274	85,016	1,120,385
14	Direct investment abroad	307,983	17,533	. . .	. . .	1,384	18,917	326,900
15	Foreign securities . .	146,713	7,846	8,507	−6,308	. . .	10,045	156,758
16	Bonds	92,044	6,937	−375	−4,579	. . .	1,983	94,027
17	Corporate stocks.	54,669	909	8,882	−1,729	. . .	8,062	62,731
18	U.S. claims on unaff. foreigners reported by U.S. nonbank firms.	31,216	1,684	. . .	. . .	. . .	1,684	32,900
19	U.S. claims reported by U.S. banks, not incl. elsewhere.	549,457	54,481	. . .	. . .	−110	54,371	603,828

Source: Bureau of Economic Analysis, *Survey of Current Business*, June 1989, p. 42.

Positon, by Area

Western Europe		Canada		Japan		Latin America and Other Western Hemisphere		Other Countries, International Organitzations and Unallocated	
1987	1988	1987	1988	1987	1988	1987	1988	1987	1988
−390,425	−436,855	53,381	53,498	−84,317	−128,489	28,852	−23,556	14,207	2,867
402,668	431,037	151,980	154,940	113,402	156,291	298,838	303,486	202,790	207,917
12,073	14,970	0	0	982	2,345	31	48	32,710	30,439
...	...	...	...	...	...	...	...	11,078	11,057
...	...	...	...	...	...	...	...	10,283	9,637
...	...	...	...	...	...	...	...	11,349	9,745
12,073	14,970	0	0	982	2,345	31	48	...	...
9,925	9,037	396	317	36	29	18,347	18,580	59,809	57,520
9,871	8,984	370	320	4	...	18,050	18,243	59,343	57,332
9,698	8,825	370	320	4	...	17,660	17,883	58,292	56,374
173	159	...	...	...	...	390	360	1,051	958
54	53	26	−3	32	29	297	337	466	187
380,670	407,030	151,584	154,623	112,384	153,917	280,460	284,858	110,271	119,957
146,243	152,232	58,377	61,244	14,671	16,868	44,905	49,283	43,787	47,273
80,111	84,888	58,572	65,489	...	...	1,182	1,070	6,848	5,310
48,218	47,362	38,613	42,926	...	...	...	...	5,213	3,739
31,893	37,526	19,959	22,563	...	...	1,182	1,070	1,635	1,571
13,693	15,125	3,913	3,624	1,767	1,540	8,927	9,196	2,916	3,415
140,623	154,785	30,722	24,266	95,946	135,509	225,446	225,309	56,720	63,959

TABLE 5–2 (Concluded)

Line	Type of Investment	Position 1987	Capital Flows (a)	Price Changes (b)	Ex-change Rate Changes (c)	Other Changes (d)	Total (a+b+c+d)	Position 1988
			Changes in Position in 1988 (Decrease (–))					
			Attributable to:					
				Valuation Adjustments				
20	Foreign assets in the United States.........	1,547,979	219,299	22,697	–1,967	–1,803	238,226	1,786,205
21	Foreign official assets in the United States	283,552	38,882	–331	...	...	38,551	322,103
22	U.S. Government securities	218,929	42,992	–2,672	...	...	40,320	259,249
23	U.S. Treasury securities.......	211,078	41,683	–2,474	...	...	39,209	250,287
24	Other	7,851	1,309	–198	...	...	1,111	8,962
25	Other U.S. Government liabilities	15,471	–1,284	...	...	...	–1,284	14,187
26	U.S. liabilities reported by U.S. banks, not included elsewhere.	31,838	–331	...	...	...	–331	31,507
27	Other foreign official assets...........	17,314	–2,495	2,341	...	...	–154	17,160
28	Other foreign assets in the United States	1,264,427	180,418	23,028	–1,967	–1,803	199,676	1,464,103
29	Direct investment in the United States ..	271,788	58,436	...	...	–1,373	57,063	328,851
30	U.S. Treasury securities	78,339	20,144	–1,857	...	...	18,287	96,626
31	U.S. securities other than U.S. Treasury securities.	344,257	26,448	24,885	–1,967	...	49,366	393,623
32	Corporate and other bonds	170,831	26,925	–603	–1,967	...	24,355	195,186
33	Corporate stocks ..	173,426	–477	25,488	...	...	25,011	198,437
34	U.S. liabilities to unaffiliated foreigners reported by U.S. nonbanking concerns.	29,404	6,558	...	...	–430	6,128	35,532
35	U.S. liabilities reported by U.S. banks, not included elsewhere.	540,639	68,832	...	...	...	68,832	609,471

Positon, by Area									
Western Europe		Canada		Japan		Latin America and Other Western Hemisphere		Other Countries, International Organitzations and Unallocated	
1987	1988	1987	1988	1987	1988	1987	1988	1987	1988
793,093	867,892	98,599	101,442	197,719	284,780	269,986	327,042	188,583	205,050
128,168	127,052	5,266	9,764	. . .	. . .	8,843	10,997	. . .	. . .
. . .	. . .	. . .	. . .	. . .	. . .	. . .	. . .	. . .	. . .
. . .	. . .	. . .	. . .	. . .	. . .	. . .	. . .	. . .	. . .
. . .	. . .	. . .	. . .	. . .	. . .	. . .	. . .	. . .	. . .
4,424	4,030	322	306	1,425	1,644	627	565	8,672	7,642
. . .	. . .	. . .	. . .	. . .	. . .	. . .	. . .	. . .	. . .
. . .	. . .	. . .	. . .	. . .	. . .	. . .	. . .	. . .	. . .
664,925	740,840	93,333	91,678	. . .	. . .	261,143	316,045	. . .	. . .
186,076	216,418	24,013	27,361	35,151	53,354	12,671	17,019	13,876	14,698
. . .	. . .	. . .	. . .	. . .	. . .	. . .	. . .	. . .	. . .
238,778	265,317	32,208	38,124	37,910	48,768	20,150	25,446	15,213	15,968
134,090	149,170	3,384	4,054	23,186	30,072	4,383	6,174	5,788	5,716
104,688	116,147	28,824	34,070	14,724	18,696	15,767	19,272	9,425	10,252
14,543	18,920	1,834	2,047	4,708	5,387	1,928	2,322	6,391	6,856
. . .	. . .	. . .	. . .	. . .	. . .	. . .	. . .	. . .	. . .

My impression is that Canadians are (unduly, in my opinion) sensitive about foreign ownership of assets in their country and about foreign influences on their culture. Of course, their view of foreigners is their prerogative, not ours. As a result of their xenophobia, they have some of the tightest foreign investment regulations among the Western industrialized nations. And they are virtually alone in disclosing the identities and financial data of foreigners who invest in their country. To the extent that these disclosure requirements reduce foreign real investment in Canada (and I am convinced that that is the case), this policy works to their detriment, not to the investors' who take their capital elsewhere.

When it reports these investment data, the BEA customarily observes that not all components are valued on a current basis and that some may be incomplete. As a result, the U.S. *International Investment Position,* at any point in time, may not be accurate. "In practice, problems in the underlying source data preclude complete coverage and consistent current valuation of assets. . . . As a result, the *IIP* is a rough indicator, not a precise measure, of U.S. assets abroad and foreign assets in the United States, and it must be used and interpreted with caution."[11]

I indicated that portfolio investments—stocks and bonds—are valued each year on a current basis. The adjustments are facilitated by the availability of financial market indexes.

By contrast, direct investment, both inward and outward, is carried at book value—that is, historical cost. Book values are used by companies here and abroad for their own financial reports, "so that, with few exceptions, book values are the only ones readily available to companies required to report in BEA surveys." The practical result is that both U.S. direct investment abroad ($327 billion at the end of 1988) and foreign direct investment here ($329 billion) are undervalued.

It is generally accepted that of the two, foreign investment here is much more recent, so that U.S. investment abroad is undervalued by a far greater amount; and that U.S.

---

[11]Ibid., p. 40.

direct investment abroad still far exceeds foreign direct investment here. This view is supported by the facts that in 1988, income on U.S. foreign direct investment amounted to $48 billion, compared with $17 billion earned by foreigners on their direct investment here. I would not, however, apply the ratio of incomes mechanically to the investment values.

Included among U.S. assets is an item, gold, valued at $11 billion. That represents our physical stock at the official treasury price of $42.22 an ounce. At the market price, the value would have been over $100 billion. Similarly, U.S. claims on unaffiliated foreigners, $33 billion, may be understated because of inadequate reporting, according to Federal Reserve analyses.

Some important adjustments could also be made in the other direction, including U.S. bank claims on foreigners, which totaled $604 billion at the end of 1988. "About three quarters consisted of claims on industrial countries and Caribbean banking centers. The rest included claims on [loans to] a number of heavily indebted developing countries, claims that are in many cases substantially discounted in secondary markets."[12] Thus, this asset is somewhat overstated compared with an up-to-date market valuation.

Another important statistic deserves mention. Perhaps it should be called an "anti-statistic"—the statistical discrepancy. In the 11 years 1978 to 1988 inclusive, the sum of the discrepancies shows an understatement of net capital inflow of about $167 billion as compared with the current account deficits. Prior to 1978, the discrepancies were smaller and largely offsetting. Most analysts regard this discrepancy as an indication of underreporting capital inflow (maybe because some of it is not only "hot" but "dirty" as well), rather than an overstatement of the current account deficit.

Even if all the statistical discrepancy is allocated to net capital inflow, it still appears that the other possible adjustments add up to a U.S. international investment position considerably better than minus $553 billion. Some people think that the negative position is half that or less. And if you

---

[12]Ibid., p. 40.

subtract foreign equity holdings from pure debt, the United States may not be a debtor nation at all. If it is, the amount is small in relation to our economy.

If the true current valuations were known, I believe they would show that the United States holds vastly more direct investments abroad than foreigners hold here. And most economists would agree, although not unanimously, that direct investment has been beneficial for our economy. It is curious, therefore, that direct investment—about 18 percent of foreign assets here—has been singled out for suspicion and criticism (generally unfounded) accompanied by demands for more restrictions. At first, the cry was "if a company sells to American consumers, then it should also create production jobs here."[13]

But it turned out that neither business nor labor interests wanted that. "Our concerns over foreign investment in U.S. assets stem, in part, from our obligation to effectively represent union members in collective bargaining."[14] Lee Iacocca, I understand, once opposed the Toyota-General Motors joint venture on the grounds that Toyota would bring along their production methods and U.S. producers could not compete with that. That is my candidate for the all-time most outrageous economic comment.

Would we be better off if we kept out better production methods? On the more humorous side—during the 1988 Presidential campaign, Michael Dukakis found himself greeting the workers in a St. Louis factory. He complained strongly about foreign company operations in the United States. It turned out that that establishment was owned by, and those workers employed by, an Italian company. (Although that was not as funny as his photograph in a helmet riding atop a tank.)

For several years, Congressman John Bryant, Democrat of Texas, has been introducing amendments or separate legislation to gain tighter control over foreign direct invest-

---

[13]Testimony of Howard D. Samuel, AFL-CIO, on disclosure of foreign investment in the United States, before the House Subcommittee of Telecommunications, Consumer Protection and Finance, May 8, 1986.

[14]Ibid.

ment in the United States. One of his important provisions calls for public disclosure of the identities and financial records of foreign individuals who invest here. In addition to some business and labor support, Bryant gained endorsements from a few academicians who, I assume, were following labor's position.

Here is one overview: "Foreign investment is changing the face of America, the lives of Americans, and the nature of our political process. A surge of foreign money is rebuilding the nation's cities, reshaping basic industries, and building manufacturing and assembly plants that are creating jobs for millions of Americans." That's *bad?* I thought that this was what America was all about. But get this: "Some of these foreign investors have hidden agendas, including the destruction of American competitors and the acquisition of American technology. . . ." No, the second quotation is not from a reincarnated Joe McCarthy.

Both passages, in fact, are adapted from a book by the Martin and Susan Tolchin family, an exaggerated, alarmist attack on foreign investment in the United States.[15] They assert that foreigners are acquiring our technology, trying to corner our markets, draining our money by repatriating most of their profits back to the parent company, compromising our national security, and infringing on our sovereignty by influencing (even "blackmailing") state and local governments and perhaps the federal government. They also support Congressman Bryant's claims that BEA data are inaccurate and that we must have public disclosure of individual financial records.

Question: How can they *know* all that if our data are no good? And they complain that "those who have ventured forth to look at the policy implications of foreign investment are often labelled protectionist, xenophobic, and racist." They have only themselves to blame for the labels. Certainly, they are protectionist. If they are not xenophobic, it can only be because they do not really mean what they say. I do not think

---

[15]Testimony of Susan Tolchin before the Senate Committee on the Budget, March 22, 1988.

they are racist, but they are caught in the coincidence of complaining about foreigners investing here just when the investment flow is increasing rapidly from Japan. And that, I think, leaves the burden with them.

Because the data in question are collected by the BEA which was part of my office, I had the "honor" to testify against the Bryant legislation on several occasions. My opposition was and still is fourfold: It's hypocritical, discriminatory, damaging, and unnecessary. It is hypocritical because throughout the postwar period we (the U.S. government) argued to our trading partners that our investment in their countries was good for them. And so it was. It helped rebuild their economies and make them the strong competitors they are today.

It is discriminatory because it would subject foreign investors to more onerous disclosure requirements than we impose on domestic investors. This would harm foreign investors by requiring them to disclose proprietary information. In which case, many of them would pick up their marbles and play elsewhere.

Some of our business people, labor officials and their apologists would say "good." The truth is, it would be bad. We need more real investment, not less. Many U.S. corporations with production and distribution facilities in other countries probably would find themselves hurt by the same kind of retaliatory, discriminatory measures. In the end, we would find an "investment war," while more subtle, to be just as harmful as a trade war.

The proposed legislation would be damaging in two fundamental ways. One I have already indicated—it would cut down foreign real investment in the United States. When I testified to this effect, proponents of the legislation complained that I had not documented the claim. Of course, we cannot document it. So far, we have successfully avoided the damaging legislation.

What do we have to go on? Both BEA and the Census Bureau, another part of my office, have learned over many years that respondents to surveys—domestic as much as foreign—are *extremely* sensitive to disclosure of proprietary information. And both agencies have carefully developed a mutual trust with their respondents, based on the assurance that individual information will not be disclosed. I have no doubt that such disclosure would reduce investment. The only legitimate question is by how much.

The other way that disclosure of individual records would be damaging is that it would undermine the integrity and accuracy of the government's *entire* statistical system, not just the international data. Don't you think that a domestic respondent to a survey would become concerned if our government began to disclose private data, even in another area? Most of our surveys are voluntary. Would we continue to get the same degree of cooperation if respondents lost confidence in the confidentiality of their data? And even if new legislation made all surveys mandatory, would the responses be as accurate as before?

A great deal of concern has been expressed recently about the accuracy of government statistics. I believe this concern has been exaggerated. Despite budget cutbacks, the quality of our data has not deteriorated. And since I no longer have any responsibility in this area, I can say freely that taxpayers get honest and excellent value for their money from BEA, Census, and the BLS.

BEA is, roughly, a $30 million agency. It has maintained nearly all its programs despite funding losses. But some important research has been delayed. Another $2 to 3 million would do wonders there. And it does not have to raise total government spending. It can easily come out of things like a Racine marina or one of the other pork barrel projects.

Thus, it should be clear that the Bryant legislation or anything similar is a bad proposal. Not because it will hurt *us* as well as *them*. Or, in fact, hurt us *more* than them. But simply that it will hurt us, and unnecessarily. It is unnecessary because the government already has all the teeth it needs to control detrimental takeovers. Future administrations require only adequate diligence and a willingness to bite.

The Omnibus Trade Act of 1988 contains a section—the Exon provision—that empowers "the President or his designee to investigate mergers, acquisitions, or takeovers by or with foreign persons which could result in foreign control of persons engaged in interstate commerce in the United States." This provision was not the first tooth—the administration already had a mouthful. In reality, all it needs is interest, concern, and friendly persuasion. The claim of compromising national security or sovereignty is unfounded, alarmist nonsense. Disclosure legislation would add nothing of practical value.

It is also unnecessary because the voluminous data we already collect and publish are more than adequate to monitor foreign activity in the United States. BEA statistics published in annual and quarterly reports provide all the information one needs for legitimate research or policy functions. They include details of balance-of-payments transactions and capital flows and fine details on the operations of U.S. affiliates of foreign companies. Such details include: "the affiliates' total assets; net income; employment and employee compensation; sales of goods and services; U.S. merchandise exports and imports; property, plant, and equipment; and research and development expenditures. Detailed tabulations are published by industry of U.S. affiliate, by country of ultimate beneficial owner or foreign parent, and, for selected items, by state."[16]

Table 5–3 (on page 136) provides a small sample of further statistics on foreign direct investment in the United States, by industry sectors and countries of origin.[17] For 1988, the total was $329 billion. The largest industry component was manufacturing, $121 billion, or 37 percent of the total. The next largest concentration was in trade—wholesale and retail—$65 billion.

The largest investor in the United States continues to be the United Kingdom—$102 billion, nearly twice Japan's holdings of $53 billion. Britain's largest holdings are in manufacturing, while Japan's are in trade. Japan also has relatively

---

[16]Testimony of Robert Ortner before the House Subcommittee on International Economic Policy and Trade, September 22, 1988.

[17]BEA, *Survey of Current Business*, June 1989, p. 48.

large holdings in real estate. Recently, they purchased Rockefeller Center, a choice New York City property. It crossed my mind that we should have tried hard to sell them the New York City subway system instead. Who knows? Maybe they could run the system better, safer, and cheaper than New York City does. Are they taking our technology? According to Lee Iacocca, and according to numbers of patents awarded, they are bringing at least as much as they are getting.

Are foreigners buying up and taking over America, as the isolationists claim? The evidence shows that their holdings are relatively small. As I said earlier, this is a large country. As far as land is concerned, it is generally agreed that foreign holdings amount to less than 1 percent, and probably closer to half of 1 percent.

For total asset values, real and financial, estimates differ by several percentage points. Interestingly, the variation does not result from disagreement over the value of foreign holdings—the BEA data are generally accepted as accurate—but it occurs because we do not have adequate, comparable statistics for U.S. total wealth. The Federal Reserve has made some estimates, using BEA tangible asset data, plus their valuations of financial assets. On this basis, it appears that foreign holdings amount to something in the range of 3 to 5 percent of U.S. wealth.[18] These kinds of estimates should be treated with caution, however, pending further research.

Nonetheless, that "guesstimate" range is supported by hard evidence from employment data. BEA recently reported the results of a complete benchmark survey covering 1987 data for U.S. nonbank affiliates of foreign companies. In 1987, these affiliates employed 3.6 percent of all workers in U.S. nonbank businesses.[19] That share represents a modest increase from 2.7 percent in 1980, the last time a benchmark survey was conducted, and a modest portion of total U.S. employment in 1987. That is hardly a sign that foreign businesses are taking over America.

---

[18]See, for example, *Economic Report of the President,* January 1989, p. 130.
[19]BEA, *Survey of Current Business,* July 1989, p. 130.

TABLE 5-3
Foreign Direct Investment Position in the United States at Yearend
[Million of dollars]

	1987								
	All Indus-tries	Petro-leum	Manu-facturing	Trade	Bank-ing	Fi-nance, except Bank-ing	Insur-ance	Real Estate	Other Ser-vices
All countries..........	271,788	35,598	94,745	50,009	14,455	3,828	17,392	27,516	28,245
Canada................	24,013	1,426	7,636	3,626	1,354	484	2,588	4,417	2,483
Europe	186,076	32,957	73,981	27,926	6,759	5,403	13,673	10,379	14,999
European Communities (12)	165,427	32,604	62,400	24,803	6,587	4,227	11,764	9,850	13,192
Belgium	2,638	(D)	701	412	32	(D)	0	13	(D)
France	10,119	(D)	8,567	656	648	-661	124	57	(D)
Germany, Federal Republic of........	20,315	148	9,294	6,170	367	649	1,630	1,143	914
Italy	1,707	(D)	245	482	428	30	(D)	(D)	(D)
Luxembourg.........	133	(D)	50	(D)	6	-16	0	16	2
Netherlands	49,115	(D)	16,137	4,085	2,518	2,586	3,861	3,311	(D)
United Kingdom......	79,669	(D)	27,061	12,480	2,022	(D)	6,106	5,140	7,969
Other Europe.........	20,649	352	11,580	3,123	172	1,176	1,909	530	1,807
Sweden	4,953	351	3,133	1,211	(D)	-167	(D)	7	(D)
Switzerland	14,686	200	7,996	1,672	(D)	1,216	1,618	391	(D)
Japan	35,151	-2	5,345	15,678	3,513	2,115	(D)	6,098	(D)
Australia, New Zealand, and South Africa	6,552	95	3,040	200	28	-29	(D)	329	(D)
Latin America and other Western Hemisphere....	12,671	748	3,556	2,262	1,807	-4,164	931	4,802	2,729
South and Central America	4,394	243	484	281	1,705	52	(D)	284	(D)
Panama	2,319	(D)	542	174	(D)	41	(D)	151	16
Other	2,075	(D)	-58	107	(D)	11	(D)	134	(D)
Other Western Hemisphere.........	8,277	505	3,072	1,981	102	-4,216	(D)	4,518	(D)
Bermuda	1,712	238	250	(D)	0	(D)	(D)	250	(D)
Netherlands Antilles...	9,317	190	2,345	1,118	(D)	215	(D)	3,588	1,764
U.K. Islands, Caribbean.........	-3,148	(D)	448	161	(D)	-4,809	0	509	(D)
Other	396	(D)	29	(D)	0	(D)	0	171	(D)
Middle East............	4,998	(D)	263	79	610	187	0	870	(D)
Isreal	514	0	(D)	(D)	404	(D)	0	1	-8
Other...............	4,484	(D)	(D0	(D)	206	(D)	0	868	(D)
Other Africa, Asia, and Pacific	2,325	(D)	924	238	384	-168	10	621	(D)
Addendum—OPEC.......	4,897	(D)	181	149	356	9	0	837	(D)

D Suppressed to avoid disclosure of data of individual companies.

Source: Bureau of Economic Analysis, *Survey of Current Business*, June 1989, p. 48.

All Indus-tries	Petro-leum	Manu-facturing	Trade	Bank-ing	Fi-nance, except Bank-ing	Insur-ance	Real Estate	Other Ser-vices
328,850	34,704	121,434	64,929	17,453	2,124	20,252	31,929	36,024
27,361	1,614	9,391	3,513	1,458	600	2,993	4,169	3,624
216,418	31,536	91,932	36,709	9,099	2,417	15,812	10,532	18,380
193,912	31,169	79,525	32,898	8,804	1,745	13,535	10,016	16,220
4,024	(D)	989	695	34	56	0	12	(D)
11,364	(D)	9,908	520	687	−764	139	95	(D)
23,845	172	13,268	6,851	293	−626	1,776	1,079	1,034
667	(D)	107	515	446	(D)	(D)	(D)	(D)
525	(D)	346	(D)	12	15	0	10	46
48,991	(D)	17,153	5,153	2,729	3,190	4,685	3,340	(D)
101,909	18,779	37,021	18,647	3,669	870	6,863	5,323	10,737
22,505	367	12,407	3,811	295	671	2,277	517	2,160
5,263	395	3,618	1,482	(D)	(D)	(D)	13	(D)
15,896	92	8,072	2,083	(D)	1,411	1,935	388	(D)
53,354	−79	12,222	18,736	3,895	2,863	(D)	10,017	(D)
5,624	287	2,279	419	11	−838	(D)	416	(D)
17,019	898	4,221	3,934	1,942	−3,108	1,150	5,217	2,766
4,978	446	406	326	1,845	47	(D)	338	(D)
2,747	6	501	209	(D)	46	(D)	216	77
2,232	440	−95	116	(D)	1	(D)	122	(D)
12,040	452	3,815	3,608	97	−3,154	(D)	4,878	(D)
1,680	107	328	(D)	0	(D)	−113	242	99
10,591	264	3,118	2,084	83	153	(D)	3,190	(D)
−1,104	(D)	355	200	14	−3,658	1	1,354	(D)
873	(D)	13	(D)	0	(D)	2	92	47
5,831	(D)	281	910	657	216	0	923	(D)
519	0	(D)	(D)	433	(D)	0	1	−7
5,312	(D)	(D)	(D)	224	(D)	0	922	(D)
3,243	(D)	1,109	709	390	−26	8	655	(D)
6,221	745	571	(D)	363	26	0	879	(D)

The data also show that affiliates' activity was heavily concentrated in manufacturing firms. Of all workers employed by foreign-owned companies, 48 percent worked for manufacturers, over twice the U.S. average. Retail and wholesale trade employed about 28 percent of affiliates' workers, and services, 9 percent. By country of ultimate beneficial ownership, British-owned firms employed 20 percent of the workers; Canadian-owned firms about the same; German, 12 percent; Japanese and Dutch, 9 percent each; and French and Swiss, 6 percent each.

In the manufacturing sector, the foreign share can be measured readily by employment, assets, and sales. In 1987, U.S. affiliates of foreign firms employed over 7 percent of all manufacturing workers. The two largest employers were the petroleum and chemical industries, which employed 40 percent and 24 percent, respectively. Obviously, affiliates in a number of industries had less than the 7 percent average.

At the same time, these affiliates owned 13 percent of all manufacturing assets. The two largest holdings were in stone, clay, and glass products and in chemical companies. By countries, Canada and the United Kingdom controlled the most assets, with about $50 billion each; then Germany, $28 billion; France, $16 billion; and Switzerland and Japan, about $15 billion each.

That the shares indicated by employment and by assets do not precisely match is not an indication of inconsistency or inaccuracy in any of the data. Different industries have varying degrees of labor-intensity; it appears that foreign assets are more heavily concentrated in industries with lower labor factors.

One purpose in citing a few of these figures is to indicate the enormous amount of data available. The few figures listed do not even qualify as the tip of the iceberg. We know which countries are the ultimate beneficial owners of how much in which industries. These data, plus additional individual reports from many other sources, provide the president with all the information he needs to protect our national interests, and he has all the authority he needs to do so.

In the light of this information, the claim that foreigners are trying to corner our markets is ridiculous. Foreign investors are subject to more scrutiny than domestic investors are. Besides, our antitrust laws apply equally to them in their operations here. Even in the two industries where they own close to one third of the assets, there is no evidence that they are gaining monopoly control.

If foreigners want to invest here, are we not better off if they put their money into plant and equipment? Would you prefer that they keep it sloshing around the stock and bond markets? Wall Street does not need any more help in that direction.

There are benefits of foreign direct investment here. One is employment. While foreign investors' share is a modest 3.6 percent, it still comes to over three million jobs. In 1987, they paid these workers $94 billion in compensation.

Critics complain that the affiliates repatriate most of their earnings. Would you like to know how much their total earnings were in 1987? Less than $10 billion—just slightly more than 10 percent of the compensation they paid to American workers. In 1987, their earnings amounted to less than a 4 percent return on investment. In 1988, they did slightly better, lifting the return to 5.6 percent—still a modest rate.

The 1987 benchmark data also show that these affiliate companies invested $31.6 billion in new plant and equipment, up 11 percent from their 1986 expenditures. American companies increased their investment less than 3 percent in 1987. And to those of you who still think that budget deficits are our number one problem, you may be comforted to know that U.S. affiliates of foreign companies paid taxes here in substantial amounts in 1987: a total of nearly $10 billion in taxes on incomes to federal, state, and local governments and another nearly $20 billion in sales and property taxes, excise, import and export duties, and other payments.

Is there no drawback to the foreign operations here? Well, no one is perfect. So far, they are adding to our trade deficit—or so it appears. In 1987, U.S. affiliates of foreign companies exported $48 billion in merchandise but imported

$141 billion worth of goods. Many of these imports consist of parts for local assembly. Hopefully, the record will improve in coming years.

According to one view:

> Foreign companies must learn to walk on American soil before they can run. Typically they start conservatively, relying on trusted sources back home to provide most of the parts for American assembly. Only after they have trained managers, taken the measure of the local work force, and tested local suppliers with small orders, do they bet the reputation of the company on a product that is largely American.[20]

I say it appears that the affiliates are adding to our trade deficit, but we cannot be sure of that. Suppose that they were assembling the products at home. Would we still be buying them? If so, our imports would be even larger. And if they were not here exporting finished goods back home, would American companies be exporting that additional amount? Probably not.

In any case, their assembly operations here provide an opportunity. In 1985 and 1986 the dollar was still high. We are cost competitive now. We have to become price and quality competitive. If they still insist on parts from home, their competitors here—American companies—will have cost advantages, which *should* mean more business here if not abroad.

One way or another—in fact in many ways—they have come, they're here, and they're here to stay. Like it or not, the United States is part of the world's economy, and the world is part of us. And these relationships will grow with an irresistible force, despite the best (or worst) efforts of the trade and investment protectionists. These relationships will grow because they are to the benefit of all countries and to the benefit of the vast majority of people in them.

I argued earlier that our investment abroad has been beneficial to the host countries. But that is not why we are

---

[20]Economic Scene, *New York Times,* November 8, 1989, p. D2.

there. Our corporations invest abroad because they believe it to be to *their* advantage. Similarly, foreigners do not invest here for philanthropic reasons—neither private individuals nor governments. We did not "beg, borrow, or steal." They are here voluntarily and even enthusiastically. I believe that the direct investment has been beneficial to us as well as to them.

But all of the foreign investment here—real and financial—does not mean we are a debtor nation in the same sense that the Latin American countries are. We have not borrowed foreign currencies, except privately in relatively small amounts, and that is offset by foreign lending. We have virtually no scheduled repayments due to foreigners, apart from domestic financial arrangements—and those we would have whether foreigners participated in them or not. And we are certainly not dependent on foreign capital.

If we have a debt burden, it is domestic. And here, we do have problems. Witness the recent failures among thrift institutions and retail firms. Our tax system encourages borrowing. And it has been greatly enlarged by the takeover and leveraged buyout craze. During the next recession, or even the current slowdown, some of this "junk" will not be repaid. Foreigners may then share in the losses. But our ability or failure to repay any part of these loans is a domestic affair. It does not matter who holds the debt—Americans or foreigners.

What if foreign investors become disillusioned, then, and decide to leave? This gets to the heart of whether foreigners have control over us. They have virtually no loans to call. They cannot pick up the factories, hotels, and office buildings and take them home. But some of them threaten that they will not go on financing our economy forever.

This is one of the issues raised in a recent book published in Japan by Messrs. Morita and Ishihara, *The Japan That Can Say No*. In a lengthy review of the book, Professor Lawrence Summers observes:

> So far the Japanese have used their financial power to stabilize the United States and world economies. At the insistence of the Japanese Ministry of Finance, Japanese insurance companies and other financial institutions lost tens

of billions of dollars trying to stabilize the dollar's decline in 1986 and 1987. These losses represent a larger outlay than all of America's postwar assistance to Japan, even after allowance for price inflation. But they may not always be so generous. . . . If Japanese investors were to stop rolling over their investments in Treasury bills and certificates of deposit, the dollar would go into free fall.[21]

If this is what Morita and Ishihara are threatening, don't worry, they're bluffing. There is nothing to the Samurai sword-rattling. In no way are they trying to support the dollar to help us. That is not what they are doing. They are supporting the dollar to protect their investments already here, to protect their trade surplus with the United States and the rest of the world, and to protect the profit margins of their domestic manufacturers who export to the United States. *That* is what they are doing.

Table 5–2 shows that Japan held $285 billion in assets in the United States at the end of 1988. Each 1 percent decline in the dollar relative to the yen would mean a loss of nearly $3 billion to Japanese investors. It would also mean the loss of competitive advantages that Japanese manufacturers enjoy here. If the yen rises, and Japanese manufacturers try to hold down the dollar price of their goods, it would mean cutting their profit margins and, at some point, suffering losses.

It would also accelerate the improvement already underway in the U.S. trade balance. As that becomes evident, and long before we move into surplus, private investors around the world will begin to move into dollars.

One final point to remember—it is no threat or ultimatum, just a fact of economic life: Foreigners as a group, *cannot* have it both ways. They cannot both not have our dollar assets and not "eat" our goods. While our current account is in deficit, they *will* take and hold our dollar payments. If they wish to become net liquidators instead of net investors, they *must* take our goods.

---

[21]Tough Talk From Tokyo, *New York Times,* December 3, 1989, Business section, p. 2.

This does not mean that either way we are winners. So far, we are not doing too well in a variety of ways, domestically and internationally. We have to become more competitive. International trade and investment is a game our trading partners and competitors are more experienced in than we are. We are more like raw rookies. We would be better advised to become good at it, and as quickly as possible, than to keep whining and sniveling about it—sniveling about foreign barriers and subsidies and foreigners buying too much of our property.

The New York Mets baseball team joined the National League in 1962 with players who were, let us say, less than strongly competitive. And by *competitive* I mean genuinely good—just as I would use the term in reference to the United States economy. The team launched its maiden season with a disastrous series of losses. Whereupon the manager, Casey Stengel, called a team meeting. If you do not know who Casey Stengel was, he was a colorful character somewhat in the Yogi Berra mold (although he preceded Yogi). If you do not know who Yogi is, I cannot help you.

Anyway, Casey reportedly opened the meeting with the question, "Is there anyone here who knows how to play this game?" What he said afterward was not reported; and if it was, it probably could not be repeated here. But no matter, the team proceeded to lose 120 games that year (out of 160 played), a twentieth century record. Needless to say, they finished last in the league and were last in batting, fielding, and pitching.

The team's management then undertook to build a winner. I suppose if Congressmen Gephart and Bryant ran the club, building a winner would have meant eliminating cheating on the other teams (you know, tampering with the ball, stealing signs, corking bats, and so on) and keeping foreigners off the Mets. And if they had been successful, other teams would have given up all cheating, the Mets would have had no foreigners on the team, and they would still be in last place. But they did become competitive (good) quickly (with new players) and won the world championship in 1969, becoming known as the "Miracle Mets."

Sure, baseball isn't exactly economics. But there is enough similarity to teach us a lesson. Our incomes and standards of living in the long run depend on how good we are and not on whether we stop foreign cheating and keep foreign investment out of America.

Chapter Six

AMERICA, THE COMPETITOR: BECOMING GOOD

Myth: We have to raise saving.
Fact: We have to raise investment.
Investment equals saving but
they're not the same thing.

During the mid-1980s, as the trade deficit was reaching its crescendo, the notion of competitiveness struck Washington's official community. For a short while, it was the biggest, flashiest, brassiest bandwagon in town. Everyone jumped on. After all, who could be against "competitiveness?" It sounded almost as good as motherhood, apple pie, and the American flag (except to the few "sickies" who take some pleasure in burning it). The parade passed by quickly, however, because there was little, if any, political gain to be had. How could there be? *Everyone* from both parties was in favor of it. So they let it go.

They never really got as far as debating, let alone agreeing on, what competitiveness is. And how do you know when you have it? It seemed to have a strong international flavor and to imply something about being better than the other guy without saying how. Often, it just came down to having a trade surplus or at least a trade balance. A *surplus* means a country is doing more international business than its trading partners, or competitors, are. That often, but not always, suggests superiority in some competitive factors: product quality, costs, marketing and distribution, or some combination of factors.

A joke that circulated through Washington around that time went something like this: Two hikers are going through the north woods. One sees a bear in the distance running toward them. He alerts the second hiker, who immediately sits down and begins to put on his running shoes. The first says, "You're crazy, you can't outrun a bear." The second answers, "I don't have to outrun the bear, I only have to outrun you." I guess that is competitiveness with a macabre twist, but I do not think it describes exactly what we are looking for. After all, if Hiker One cannot run very well for some reason, he may be very unfortunate in this instance, but that doesn't mean that Hiker Two is a good runner. And outrunning other people may not be the only thing that matters.

In Chapter 1, I noted that countries in Eastern Europe and a number of less developed countries have trade surpluses. In many cases, they are depressing their already poor and/or inefficient economies in order to hold down imports and be able to service foreign debts. That does not make them more "competitive" than we are. Nor would we become more competitive, in any reasonable sense of the term, by raising import barriers or by depressing our economy. Either way, we could lower imports, but we would not improve our basic performance. These "solutions" to our trade problems would make us less competitive in the long run. We could also undertake to "buy in" a trade balance or surplus with an ever declining currency to make up for rising costs. I would not call that "competitiveness" either. However one approaches the question, I think it is impossible to avoid the notions of quality and efficiency—of being *good.*

Trade is a symptom of competitiveness—not always a *reliable* one, especially in the short run, and certainly not the *only* one. In an interesting article, Messrs. Hatsopoulos, Krugman, and Summers suggest that a good definition of competitiveness would be a country's ability to balance trade "while achieving an acceptable rate of improvement in its standard of living."[1] And further, "We would not view the United States as competitive unless it is able in the long run

---

[1]George N. Hatsopoulos, Paul R. Krugman, and Lawrence H. Summers, "U.S. Competitiveness: Beyond the Trade Deficit," *Science,* July 15, 1988, pp. 299–307.

to maintain a rate of growth in living standards that keeps pace with that of the rest of the world." We certainly kept pace from 1982 to 1988. We grew with the best of them, including Japan, and faster than the rest. But obviously not with balanced foreign trade.

Between the quoted statements, the authors comment that "rising living standards can be achieved through growing trade deficits (as in the United States since 1981)." Maybe I misunderstand their use of the word *through*. If they mean *because of*, they have it backwards. Our trade deficit grew in part because of our rising living standards (GNP and incomes); and the rising trade deficit served, in turn, to *slow* our growth, not to increase it.

The authors discuss living standards in terms of real incomes. I think that is correct. It is a far superior measure to consumption, used by Lawrence et al.[2] If we elect to add to our wealth as well as consume, that does not make us poorer.

The relationship between living standards and the trade balance illustrates the difficulty of defining even a simple (at least on the surface) notion like competitiveness. If our economic growth accelerates, and our standards of living (real incomes) improve along with it—especially relative to our trading partners—and if nothing else changes ("other things equal," as economists like to say), our trade balance will worsen. Certainly, the answer to that kind of trade problem is not to lower our standards of living.

There are a number of things we can try to do while still encouraging economic growth. First, foremost, and well over half the battle, we must improve productivity growth. Our excellent recovery and expansion from 1982 to 1988 was mainly cyclical in nature. Only to a minor degree was it productivity-driven. We grew by employing previously unused resources—both workers and factories. Productivity growth, at least in manufacturing, improved slightly, but the improvement may be temporary. If we succeed in moving

---

[2]Robert E. Litan et al., eds., *American Living Standards*. (Washington D.C.: The Brookings Institution, 1988).

productivity gains to a faster lane, a faster rate of economic expansion will be sustainable. Productivity growth underlies the improvement in our standards of living.

It does more than that. Productivity growth offsets wage increases and thereby holds down costs and prices, thus strengthening price-competitiveness for an individual company, an industry, or the entire economy. And how do we stack up? Table 6–1 compares U.S. changes in productivity and in unit labor costs with the same records for our six major competitors. The change in unit labor costs is conceptually a simple calculation: the change in hourly compensation minus the change in productivity. (Technically, the relationship is multiplicative, but this example is simpler and provides nearly the same result. The table presents the correct figures.) Thus, if compensation rises 6 percent and productivity rises 4 percent, unit labor costs rise about 2 percent (technically, 1.92 percent). If compensation rises 4 percent and productivity rises 6 percent, unit labor costs fall about 2 percent. In the table, changes in unit labor costs are measured first in each country's own currency and then in dollars.

In Chapter 1, I pointed out that our performance in productivity during most of the postwar years was poor. From 1960 to 1988, our productivity (output per hour) grew an average of 2.8 percent per year—the worst among the major industrial countries. For that period, the poor performance was centered mainly in the 1970s, a result of the oil shock and the severe recession of 1973 to 1975. The other countries held up generally better than we did, except for the United Kingdom, whose performance deteriorated more.

From 1979 to 1988, we picked up the pace to 3.3 percent, enough to join the pack—not the frontrunners, but not last either. We were "reasonably competitive" (sort of like "gentleman's C" grades in college).

Back in the 1970s (I cannot remember exactly when), an English economist friend asked me if I had ever visited a Japanese automobile plant. I told him I had not, but assumed they were modern and efficient. He said that was true; but that was not what impressed him during a recent visit. What was really impressive, he said, was that the workers were

TABLE 6–1
Output per Hour, Manufacturing, 1960–1988 (*Average Annual Rates of Change*)

Country or Area	1960–88	1960–73	1973–88	1973–79	1979–88	1979–86	1987	1988
Output per Hour								
United States	2.8	3.2	2.5	1.4	3.3	3.3	3.4	3.2
Canada	3.3	4.5	2.2	2.1	2.2	2.1	2.4	3.2
Japan	7.8	10.3	5.7	5.5	5.8	5.2	7.8	7.6
France	4.9	6.4	3.7	4.6	3.1	3.0	1.2	5.3
Germany	4.4	5.8	3.3	4.3	2.6	2.5	1.3	4.6
Italy	5.5	6.4	4.7	5.7	4.1	4.5	2.5	2.9
United Kingdom	3.7	4.2	3.3	1.2	4.7	4.4	6.4	4.9
Unit Labor Costs: National Currency Basis								
United States	3.2	1.8	4.5	8.0	2.2	2.9	-1.2	.3
Canada	4.4	1.6	7.0	9.8	5.2	5.8	2.7	2.9
Japan	3.1	4.3	2.1	6.9	-1.0	-.3	-5.1	-2.1
France	6.1	3.4	8.5	11.2	6.7	8.4	3.3	-1.6
Germany	3.9	4.3	3.6	4.9	2.7	3.2	2.6	-.5
Italy	8.6	5.5	11.4	15.9	8.5	9.9	3.8	3.4
United Kingdom	7.5	4.8	9.9	18.0	4.8	5.7	.0	2.9
Unit Labor Costs: U.S. Dollar Basis								
United States	3.2	1.8	4.5	8.0	2.2	2.9	-1.2	.3
Canada	3.6	1.3	5.5	6.9	4.6	3.3	7.7	10.9
Japan	7.0	6.6	7.3	10.8	5.0	3.5	10.4	10.5
France	5.3	4.2	6.4	12.0	2.8	1.1	19.0	-.8
Germany	7.2	8.0	6.5	11.6	3.2	.7	23.8	1.8
Italy	5.8	6.0	5.6	9.2	3.2	1.1	19.4	2.9
United Kingdom	5.8	3.7	7.6	15.2	2.7	.3	11.7	11.8

Source: U.S. Department of Labor, Bureau of Labor Statistics, June 1989.

actually *running* from one place to another, assembling the cars. "And what are they doing at British Leyland?" I asked. "They're *walking*—the picket lines," he said.

Of course, productivity measures what you actually produce. And the United Kingdom certainly got its act together under Margaret Thatcher. During the 1980s, their productivity growth was second to, and not too far from, Japan's. If they return to their class struggle after she leaves office, the record could revert to the pattern of the 1970s.

Since 1960, Italy has had the second-best productivity gains. That translates into above-average growth in GNP, incomes, and standards of living—a strongly competitive record. One might think that its productivity record also translates into international business competitiveness, but it does not. Italy's hourly compensation costs rose an average of 14.6 percent per year, fastest by far of the group. As a result, their unit labor costs (middle panel of the table) rose 8.6 percent per year, also the fastest of the group. To keep the country from being priced out of world markets, the lira had to fall. From 1960 to 1988, it declined by slightly more than half, or about 2.6 percent per year, relative to the dollar. On a dollar basis (bottom panel of the table), Italy's unit labor costs rose 5.8 percent per year, about the same as the United Kingdom's.

Japan's superior productivity performance accommodated large compensation increases for its workers, averaging over 11 percent a year; and it still left them with the slowest rise in unit labor costs. In terms of real incomes, their productivity performance gave them the fastest rising standard of living of all these countries. From 1960 to 1988, the yen rose 180 percent, an average of nearly 4 percent per year. In dollars, therefore, Japan's unit labor costs rose 7 percent per year during these 28 years.

Because their compensation levels were very low (relative to U.S. compensation) at the beginning of the period, Japan remained strongly competitive in costs and prices throughout the period. A developing reputation for quality, style, and reliability added to their competitive position. Price isn't everything.

U.S. labor costs rose a moderate 3.2 percent a year from 1960 to 1988, actually declining slightly in the last two years. This excellent performance put us near the lead when others' costs are measured in their own currencies. And we were the absolute frontrunners when others' costs are translated into dollars. If productivity underlay this performance, I think we would all agree that the United States was indeed competitive. But we bought our cost-competitiveness with the smallest pay increases of all. Our workers did enjoy all the fruits of their labor, but there wasn't much fruit to go around. In terms of rising standards of living, we were not competitive.

Chart 6–1 displays the paths of U.S. labor costs relative to a group of 11 countries since 1973, measured in local currencies and translated into dollars.[3] Please note that both lines trace *changes* since 1973. They do not tell us what the absolute relative levels are at any point in time. Thus, on a

CHART 6–1
U.S. Manufacturing Unit Labor Costs Relative to 11 Competitors
(Index: 1973 = 100)

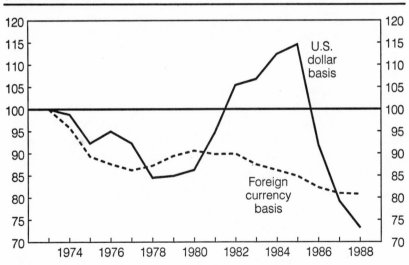

Source: Bureau of Labor Statistics

---

[3]The six foreign countries listed in Table 6–1 plus Korea, Taiwan, Denmark, The Netherlands, and Sweden.

dollar basis, the last observation at 1988 is about 73. That means that U.S. labor costs, relative to this group of 11 countries, were 27 percent lower (100 minus 73) than they were in 1973. In domestic currencies, U.S. unit labor costs declined against the others by nearly 20 percent (100 minus 80). During the 1980s, this relationship was swamped by exchange rate gyrations. The runup in the dollar from 1980 to 1985 raised our relative labor costs by more than a third. The dollar's decline from its 1985 peak lowered them, similarly, by more than a third.

Are we now labor-cost competitive? BLS data list average compensation costs for U.S. workers in manufacturing at close to $14 an hour in 1988.[4] Comparable costs, at average 1988 exchange rates, were about $13.60 in Canada and close to $13 in France, Italy, and Japan. The United Kingdom was at about $10.50, and Germany was on top with $18. The dollar's exchange value has been an important factor in bringing U.S. compensation into line with the others.

In 1985, with the dollar at its peak, U.S. compensation was at $13 an hour. Japan's, at $6.50, was half ours. German compensation, at $9.50, was also well under ours. In 1988, on average, the dollar commanded 1.76 deutsche marks, about its price in late 1989. The dollar sold for about 128 yen in 1988; and toward the end of 1989, it was about 13 percent higher at 144 yen. Thus, even with Japanese wages rising 6 percent or so faster than American, Japan maintained a general wage advantage.

Wages, however, constitute only half of the cost scissors. The other blade is productivity. The data shown in Table 6–1 refer to *growth* in productivity. What we need for this purpose are *levels*. While a number of analysts are working on such estimates, precise measures that are comparable among countries are not yet available. Meanwhile, there is a general agreement that productivity is still higher in the United States than it is among all our competitors. Therefore, unit labor costs are generally lower in the United States than they are among our major competitors.

---

[4]U.S. Department of Labor, Bureau of Labor Statistics, *International Comparisons of Hourly Compensation Costs,* Report 771, August 1989.

Thus, at the end of 1989, the United States was cost competitive. The improving trend that we have seen in U.S. foreign trade, and especially the gain in exports, is not a temporary statistical aberration. These improvements should continue into the early 1990s. But that certainly is no cause for celebration followed by all-out complacency. As in the fable of the tortoise and the hare, we raced out to an early lead after World War II. The problem is not that we are just resting or loafing now. The problem is that somewhere along the way we were transfigured into the tortoise. Our competitors are the hares; and, as I pointed out in Chapter 1, at least two of them—Japan and Canada—will catch and pass us during the 1990s.

This is not a dire warning. None of our competitors is the bear in my earlier anecdote. When they pass us, you will feel no physical pain. The only pain there *might* be, and perhaps *should* be, will come from the knowledge that we are "second rate" because we did not do our best. In this regard, we are not competitive.

This race is not a trivial matter of a social sporting event. Remember, we are talking about our standard of living. In her travels through Wonderland, Alice learned that in the Kingdom of the Queen of Hearts she had to run as fast as she could just to stay in the same place. For us, running as fast as we can will keep us abreast of our competitors. That will raise our living standards faster than our current tortoise pace.

How can we do that? For many years, economists have used simple growth concepts such as $g = s/c$; g is the economy's growth rate, s is the proportion of total income in the economy that is saved and c is the economy's ratio of its stock of capital to its output.[5] The capital-output ratio is the inverse of capital's earnings yield, or its productivity. It is something like Wall Street's price-earnings ratio. For example: suppose that capital invested in our economy earns 20 percent, or 0.20; c, then, equals 5. And if we save 10 percent of our income or output, g will be equal to $10/5$, or 2. That is, our growth rate

<hr>

[5]See, for example, R. F. Harrod, *Towards a Dynamic Economics,* (London: MacMillan, 1948), p. 77.

will be 2 percent per year. In this relationship, it is evident that if we can raise the "saving rate" to 20 percent, we can thereby raise the economy's growth rate to 4 percent. That is why economists are always talking about promoting more saving.

In this simplistic model, no distinction is made between saving and investment. They are the same thing. $g = \%$ is consistent with the accounting identity, saving equals investment ($S = I$) in our national income (GNP) accounts. Why does $S = I$? By definition, $S = Y - C$ (saving equals income less consumption) and $I = O - C$ (investment equals output less consumption). Since someone, an individual or a business, earns income for all the output, $Y = O$. Hence, $S = I$.

This is an "ex post" (after the fact), nonoperational identity. At the end of each period, in boom, depression, or war, $S = I$. They were equal in 1933, 1945, 1989, and all the years in between. Nothing in the relationship tells you how they reached those levels.

A second point worth emphasizing is the definitional content of consumption and investment. Everything purchased by consumers is "consumption," including cars and computers. Business purchases are "investment," including cars, computers, and other machinery and equipment. Business investment also includes increases in inventories of raw materials, work in process, and unsold finished goods. All government spending is included in consumption, whether it is for current salaries, office supplies, computers, cars, roads, buildings, airports, or aircraft carriers.

Economists who complain about low U.S. saving usually base their argument on our GNP data as defined in this way. In an excellent speech, Professor Robert Eisner pointed out that the problem is exaggerated. Our saving (or investment) is not actually as low as these data suggest. One of the main reasons is that we exclude government investment and household durables like cars. Sources cited by Eisner attribute three to five percentage points of the difference between U.S. and Japanese saving (investment) ratios to the fact that Japan includes government investment in its totals. Eisner suggests that we include intangible investment as well—education, training, and research and development.[6]

In a similar way, Professors Lipsey and Kravis argue in another study that we should define investment in this broader context. If we did, we would find that "the U.S. has been investing a proportion of its gross domestic product that is not far below that of other developed countries over the past decade and a half (1970–1984). Thus, the U.S. has not been a particularly extravagant nation."[7] Within this broader measure of investment, the authors observed that Japan devoted a larger share than we do to the more conventional forms of plant and equipment.

Nonetheless, while "not far below," we *are* below—we are dead last! Charts 6–2 and 6–3 compare U.S. investment performance with that of France, Germany, Japan, and the United Kingdom. Chart 6–2 shows growth in the amount of capital stock per worker against growth in productivity. It is not surprising to see, from country to country, that the faster the growth in capital per worker, the faster the growth in productivity. Chart 6–3 shows a similar relationship between the average share of investment in each country's GDP with growth in each country's productivity.

The reason that the patterns of relationship are similar is that the larger the share of output devoted to investment, the faster the stock of capital (per worker) grows. Either way you look at it, we are still last. Capital spending is not the only factor that affects changes in productivity, but these relationships across countries suggest that it explains an extremely large part of those changes.

Professor Robert M. Solow was awarded the Nobel Prize, justifiably, for his pioneering work in the analysis of sources of economic growth, or growth accounting. Others followed his approach in estimating the effects of investment on output. Generally, their models indicated that a 1 percent increase in

[6]Robert Eisner, "Presidential Address before the American Economic Association, December 29, 1988," *The American Economic Review,* March, 1989, p. 1.

[7]Robert E. Lipsey and Irving B. Kravis, "Is the U.S. a Spendthrift Nation?" National Bureau of Economic Research, Working Paper No. 2274.

CHART 6-2
Productivity and Capital/Labor, Manufacturing 1964 to 1985 (Average Annual Rates of Change)

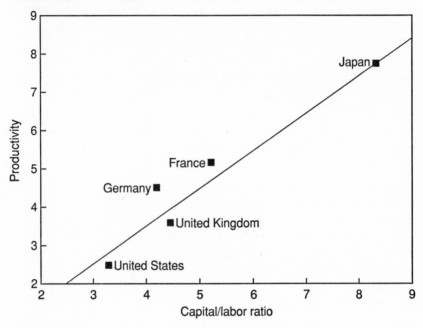

Source: OECD

investment would raise output by considerably less than 1 percent. These estimates are contradicted by the relationship shown in Charts 6–2 and 6–3. Intercountry changes appear to be proportional; that is, a one percentage point rise in capital per worker is accompanied by about a one percentage point gain in output per worker. This kind of contradiction between theory and empirical evidence is not unusual in the evolution of economic thought. But at this point, the issue is—as Groucho Marx once put it (or was it Chico?)—"Who ya gonna believe, me or your own eyes?"

I recommend that you believe your own eyes—the relationships in the charts. There are some valid reasons that the growth accounting models are understating the effects of investment on growth in output and productivity. Joan Robinson, the eminent British economist, wrote some time ago that "technical progress and the availability of natural re-

CHART 6–3
Manufacturing Productivity and Investment/GDP Ratio

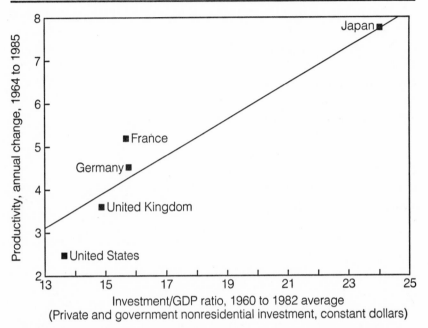

Source: OECD

sources had evidently been strong enough to make nonsense of predictions based on diminishing returns."[8]

Hatsopoulas et al. observed that "capital investment embodies technical change. Countries where the rate of investment is high are likely also to have more modern capital stocks."[9] Thus, a continuing process of investment both adds additional capital and replaces existing capital stock with new equipment that is more productive than the old. The resulting gain in output, therefore, is greater than might be expected only from replacements of and additions to capital stock. The authors also note that the relationship between capital accumulation and growth rates holds over a sample of

---

[8]Joan Robinson, *Economic Philosophy* (Chicago: Aldine Publishing Co., 1962). p. 103.
[9]Hatsopoulos et al., "U.S. Competitiveness."

115 countries. In terms of aggregate investment and output, a sample that large must come close to covering the universe.

My purpose in discussing the effects of investment on economic growth is not to join an argument already in progress. Rather, it is to point out that it will not require 5 to 10 percent growth rates in capital stock to add only one percentage point to our economic growth. If the relationship is anywhere near one-to-one, we *can* lift our growth by a significant amount if we choose to do so.

To do so, we must raise the saving and investment share of our economic output. The relationship in Chart 6–3 promises a worthwhile payoff. What is the route, saving or investment? Most economists—mainly the academicians—perhaps influenced by the Harrod and other growth models, speak of the need to raise saving.

At the beginning of the chapter, I referred to the need to raise saving to improve competitiveness as a myth. Why, if saving equals investment? Because in the real world, changes in saving or investment will have vastly different effects on the economy. They are not the same thing *operationally*. What it comes down to, is that you cannot raise saving by raising saving.

Joan Robinson noted that Harrod's growth formula, couched in terms of saving:

> leaves out of account the most important element in the whole affair—the decisions governing the rate of accumulation of capital. In a private-enterprise economy decisions to invest are taken in the light of prospective profits, and . . . prospective profits are depressed, not increased, by thrifty individuals refraining from expenditure for consumption. Thrift, in itself, is a deflationary, depressive factor in a market economy.[10]

Earlier, I quoted Robert Eisner, who questioned whether Lee Iacocca would build more factories if people suddenly saved more and bought fewer of his cars. The answer is obviously no. What happens in Iacocca's, or any other busi-

---

[10]Robinson, *Economic Philosophy,* p. 105.

ness, is that an increase in consumer saving *does* raise investment in the first instance. But it is investment in business inventories, and involuntary at that. The next step in the process is a cutback in production, enough to both eliminate the unwanted inventories and keep pace with the lower level of sales. Then come layoffs, lower incomes, and sooner or later, *lower* saving and *lower* investment (remember, they are equal). This is a fairly common type of cyclical change in our economy.

To you business people who have painfully experienced these swings and are wondering why I'm wasting your time describing such an obvious sequence of events, please bear with me. Apparently, some academicians do not understand this. Business economists, the ones on the daily real-world firing line, do understand it. You will be better advised to take your economic intelligence (oxymoron?) from them.

The way to raise saving and investment is to raise investment. I will make one concession to promoting saving, but only as an adjunct to promoting investment, and only periodically. Every five or six years, the economy approaches a business-cycle peak. High operating rates begin to generate inflationary pressures. At such times—and 1990 is one of them—it is difficult to raise activity, even through investment, without also raising inflation. Adding investment incentives, or reducing disincentives, therefore, should be accompanied by reduced spending (or reduced growth) in other areas. That is to ensure that real resources will be available for production of the new investment before the new capacity begins to add to output. But even at these times, the focus must remain on investment. Pushing only saving will turn the economic peak into the next trough.

Economic textbooks teach us that, theoretically, investment will rise if its profitability exceeds the cost of financing it. In the real world, estimating prospective profitability years into the future is extremely hazardous. Future earnings are discounted heavily because of the uncertainty of achieving them and because the cost of capital is high. In practice, business firms make their investment plans on the basis of current business conditions, the need for additional capacity, and their degree of confidence regarding the near- to intermediate-term future.

Current business operating rates have a strong influence on business investment activity. Investment usually declines during—and for a time after—recessions, because businesses do not need more capacity when they are using only 70 to 75 percent of what they already have. For that reason, investment is a lagging sector of the economy. Business investment plans generally strengthen when operating rates reach 80 percent or so and when business people are confident that the economic expansion will continue. Policymakers in Washington can contribute positively to this process by promoting sustainable economic growth with good prospects for reasonable rates of return on investment.

The Tax Reform Act of 1986, which raised effective tax rates on equipment from 10 percent to 40 percent, will be detrimental to investment and to our future standards of living. Professor Lawrence R. Klein, a Nobel Laureate and pioneer in the development of econometric models, states that "tax reform was poorly structured by taking away investment incentives in the form of tax credits and accelerated depreciation. Those features should be restored as quickly as possible because physical capital formation is . . . simultaneously anti-recessionary and helpful for restoring competitiveness."[11]

Another factor in the United States that is detrimental to investment is our high cost of capital. Our interest rates are higher, even after allowing for inflation, than they are in the economies of our strongest competitors. Our producers are at an even greater disadvantage in raising equity capital. The problem for equity finance is caused by our double taxation of dividends—once when income is earned by corporations, and again when individuals receive dividends from the corporations. As a result, our tax system creates a large gap between the cost of equity finance to the corporation and the yield realized, after taxes, by investors. This gap raises the cost of

---

[11]Lawrence R. Klein, "Components of Competitiveness," Science, July 15 1988, p. 308.

equity capital to corporations because the returns offered must be attractive to investors. Therefore, it encourages relatively more debt financing.

Our real interest rates are higher than in other countries because our tax system encourages borrowing—often unproductive—for everything from home equity loans to corporate takeovers and leveraged buyouts. It will be helpful, too, if we continue to bring down the federal budget deficit. Considering the deficit in the context of making more real resources available for investment and also lowering the cost of capital strengthens the argument for spending cuts. It hardly makes sense to save our corporations from high borrowing costs to make them more competitive by taxing their earnings away in the first place.

Our high cost of capital also explains why the United States has a much shorter planning horizon than Japan does. At a 10 percent interest rate, $1 of expected earnings in the year 2000 is worth 39 cents in 1990; at a 5 percent rate, it is worth 61 cents, over 50 percent more. It is perfectly rational for U.S. business people to focus on the nearer-term future than their counterparts in Japan do. The answer is not to scold U.S. managers, it is to lower the cost of capital.

At the same time, we must restore investment incentives. To encourage the development of new technologies and, therefore, promote investment in the most scientifically advanced equipment, it is equally important to improve the incentives for research, experimentation, and development. Earlier, I indicated that the United States allocates a smaller share of its GNP to research and development than our trading partners do. If we continue to lag behind others in this respect, we are likely to find that growth in U.S. capital investment will raise productivity less than it does among our competitors.

But in their finite wisdom, the writers of the Tax Reform Act of 1986 severely curtailed existing research incentives. The tax credit was reduced from 25 percent to 20 percent. The credit applies now only to incremental outlays in excess of expenditures in the previous three years. And the definition was tightened to include only experimental research, not product development. Thus, what was formerly known as "research and development (R&D)" is now "research and experimentation (R&E)." The new provision, moreover, was written on a renewable basis, so that business planners could not rely on it.

The Reagan and Bush administrations have proposed that this tax credit be made permanent. But locking into place an inadequate research incentive, to go along with investment disincentives (high effective tax rates on equipment) and no support for product development, just will not get the job done. Exhorting business people to invest more and conduct more R&E is no substitute for an appropriate fiscal program. As a minimum, we need to go back to pre-1986 provisions.

In another direction, our performance is more encouraging. The United States devotes a larger share of its resources to education than other industrial countries do. Lipsey and Kravis found the United States to be first "by a long distance," in terms of our population's average years of higher education.[12] And in a supplement to his message to a joint session of Congress, President Bush reported that our investment in education comes to $330 billion a year at the federal, state, and local levels combined.[13] In terms of money invested and years in school, it is generally agreed that we are internationally competitive. It is also agreed that we are not competitive in the quality of our educational product.

Appropriately, Mr. Bush recommended that for the near future we focus on results rather than on additional money. Financial rewards and recognition should be based more than previously on student achievement. Our efforts in this area are worthwhile. Education enriches our lives in the broadest sense. After all, "man does not live by 'bread' alone." And a better-educated work force is a more productive work force and a higher-earning work force. Thus, investment in R&D and in education improve the payoff to productivity from

---

[12]Lipsey and Kravis, "Is the U.S. a Spendthrift Nation?"

[13]"Building A Better America," George Bush, The White House, February 9, 1989, p. 49.

investment in new plant and equipment. In the words of Wall Street, they provide the economy with a "bigger bang for the (capital spending) buck."

Improving our competitive performance requires greater efforts in other directions also. We have developed a reputation for poor-quality products in several areas. But here, too, it appears that we are making some progress. In an interesting survey, the Federal Reserve Bank of New York reviewed developments in a number of industries important to our world trade.[14] Industries with few or no quality problems include pharmaceuticals, construction equipment, consumer electronics, machine tools, aircraft, and electric power generating equipment. Steel and electronic parts have shown quality improvement.

But problems remain in paper and in automobile manufacturing. The auto industry, unfortunately, is a highly visible sector and serves to some extent as a proxy for the reputation of U.S. manufacturing in general. The *Consumer Reports 1990 Buying Guide* shows little, if any improvement in the poor repair records of American-made cars.

Now, I am neither a quality-control expert, nor an engineer, but I will offer my opinion anyway. After all, throughout my career, I have heard almost daily (weekly?), "I'm not an economist, but . . . " I do not believe for a minute that the problem lies with our workers. "They are as good as any in the world" has become a cliche because it is true. If they are not producing good cars it is because quality was not designed into the product and into the production process in the first place. Is it true that we should not buy cars assembled on a Friday or a Monday? If so, we are paying workers too much for showing up and not nearly enough for quality output.

I should think that the companies and unions have a mutual interest in this direction. Higher quality and higher productivity should mean more business, more jobs, higher pay, and higher corporate earnings. Surely, they have been at it long enough to know how to negotiate a labor contract that will produce these results.

---

[14]Federal Reserve Bank of New York, *Quarterly Review,* Spring 1988.

The federal government also might have a role to play in this matter: Back them up with genuine investment and R&D incentives so that they can get on with it. It is for everyone's good—companies, workers in the industry, and a hundred million consumers.

And while we are at it, how about designing some style into our products? Not just autos—everything. Michael Elliott, correspondent of The Economist, wrote: "My guess is that the first thing that any foreigner notices when he wants to buy an American product is its design. There can be no country in the world where so many goods look so old-fashioned and dowdy. . . . American consumers like foreign goods. That must be, in large part, because they look nice."[15]

Poor quality and design reflect sloppiness and carelessness. They mean that to be competitive we have to maintain wider price advantages, through a low dollar, low domestic prices, or both. From design to quality to productivity, good management, organization, and planning are essential. Where these problems exist, they represent industrial mediocrity at its worst.

Well, if we can get a little help from our friends—R, E&D, education, quality, style, and improved management organization—what will it take from capital spending to make us competitive in productivity growth? Looking at Charts 6–2 and 6–3, what is a reasonable goal? How about going for 5 to 6 percent productivity growth in manufacturing by the year 2000? From the empirical relationships, it looks like we would have to raise the growth rate in capital stock per worker (Chart 6–2) from its recent 3 percent to at least 5 to 6 percent; and we would have to lift fixed nonresidential investment to 20 percent of GDP by the year 2000 from its recent level of about 15 percent.

That would mean that during the 1990s investment would average a little over 17 percent of GDP and productivity growth 4 to 5 percent per year. If growth in GDP, then, averaged close to 4 percent, fixed investment would have to

---

[15]"Competitiveness" Is a Buzzword, *Washington Post,* February 15, 1987.

grow about 6.75 percent a year to reach 20 percent of GDP in the year 2000. Is that too much to try for? From 1982 to 1988, business fixed investment increased an average of 5 percent a year and some years more. Thus, it may be reaching a little, but it is feasible.

Why do it? By 2000, the underlying trend growth rate in the economy could be faster than 4 percent. And while investment would command a larger share of GDP, and consumer spending a smaller share than today, *both* would be growing faster than they are now. So would our standard of living, however you measure it. I am confident that our economy is capable of reaching this goal. But I am not confident our leaders in Washington will let it happen. The politicians are too busy with their pay raises, pork barrel handouts, protection, and tax breaks for special interests. And too many economic advisors are telling them that the budget deficit is our number one problem and that we must raise taxes. Competitiveness is too important, therefore, to leave to economists or to politicians. To whom, then? *You! You* tell *them* what you need to make your businesses genuinely tough competitors, and keep telling them. When you do not have their ears, someone else does. And if they do not listen to you, elect new officials who will.

Chapter Seven

AMERICA, THE MEDIOCRE: RETROSPECT AND PROSPECT

It isn't a myth, and it hurts to say it. Depending on how one measures economic performance, or competitiveness if you prefer, either we're mediocre now or soon will be. We are already mediocre in growth of productivity, per capita GNP, real incomes, and standards of living. Actually, in terms of intermediate- to long-term trends, we are not even mediocre; we're last! As measured by levels of per capita output and incomes, we are still on top. But it looks like we will be off that perch and possibly in third place by the end of the century.

I refer to the intermediate- to long-term trend, because our performance improved during the 1980s. It was, in fact, excellent—especially considering that the economy had been laid up with a bad case of stagflation for several years following the second oil shock in 1979. By the end of 1982, U.S. industry was operating at about 70 percent of its capacity, and unemployment exceeded 10 percent.

The inflation fever finally subsided from a 12 to 13 percent average in 1980 to near 4 percent in 1982, where it leveled off virtually for the rest of the decade. It dropped to 1 percent in 1986 when oil prices broke, but quickly rebounded to 4.5 percent when oil prices stabilized and moved higher again. In my opinion, inflation was a major disappointment in the 1980s. Even with the severe 1980 and 1981 to 1982 recessions and a 50 percent runup in the dollar which lowered import prices, we managed only to moderate inflation, not to break it.

President Reagan's tax cuts triggered the upturn that outlasted all previous peacetime expansions. The economy's low operating rate in 1982 provided ample resources for the strong rebound in all the major sectors. Most important, the revitalized economy added 17 million jobs from 1982 to 1988, after losing a million during the previous three years. It added 27 percent in real disposable income, 3.5 percent per year, after virtually no gain for three years. And it lowered the nation's poverty rate after that rate had risen steadily for five years.

These gains are ours to keep. What was produced and earned will not be taken away in the future by today's federal deficits or debt, or by our so-called foreign debt. The gains could have been even greater if we had not lost so much business because of our growing trade deficit. And the policy measures would have been better if we had not slipped up in the Tax Reform Act of 1986. Cutting back the incentives for investment and for research and development will curtail the very things we need to keep the economy and our incomes growing in the 1990s and to make the United States competitive again.

The political critics and their economic advisors have missed this point. Had they focused on the economic substance of investment and productivity, they could have made some constructive suggestions. Instead, they are concentrating on financial shadows and asserting, for political purposes, that the growth of the 1980s was done with smoke and mirrors. As a result, all they have accomplished is rewriting the three basic lies from "The check's in the mail," "I'm from the Internal Revenue Service and I'm here to help you," and "Of course I'll respect you in the morning" to: "Our budget deficit is stifling economic growth," "We're dependent on foreign capital," and "We're the world's largest debtor."

Perhaps recalling a simple principle of economics will help to cut through the tangle of confused rhetoric. If people reduce their spending and thereby increase the share of saving in their incomes, they will slow economic activity. This is true whether they are domestic consumers, governments, or foreigners. U.S. economic growth slowed in 1989, in part because consumers raised their saving rate to over 5.5 percent from 4.25 percent in 1988.

In the same way, U.S. economic activity was bolstered by reduced foreign saving here, because the latter reflected our improved trade deficit. Foreigners increased their purchases from us (our exports) more than the rise in income they earned by exporting to us (our imports). Continued shrinkage of foreign saving in the United States and of our trade deficit will mean that more and more business activity is coming back to the United States.

Lie One: "Our budget deficit is stifling economic growth." An increase in government spending raises activity—surely there is no question about that. A cut in individual tax rates also raises activity, but probably by less than the amount of the tax cut as individuals usually save part of it. Either way—by raising spending or lowering taxes (government's income)—the government lowers its saving (or raises its dis-saving). That stimulates the economy. Simple enough, isn't it? But some economists cannot handle it. They have been telling us that this deficit "absorbs" private saving. And since that leaves less private saving to finance investments, investment must shrink, and the economy cannot grow.

There are a couple of important things wrong with their analysis. First, it isn't analysis. It is what economists (often the same ones) call "ex post accounting." Remember, saving always equals investment after the fact. What they are saying is that this year's saving is not enough to finance next year's larger activity. Of course it isn't—by definition, it was barely enough to finance this year's investment. If the economy grows next year, next year's larger saving will finance next year's investment. *Will* the economy grow next year? Surely it will if, on balance, consumers, businesses, governments (federal, state, and local), and foreigners raise their spending in the United States; and if the Federal Reserve Board is willing to accommodate some growth in money and credit.

Second, referring to saving as the "financier of business activity" substantially understates the amount of finance actually available. This measure of saving is derived from the

national income and product accounts. It is output not con-
sumed. Certainly, if consumers earn income they do not
spend, that saving is available to buy stocks, bonds, CDs,
whatever. But more finance than that is available, not only
from other sectors of the economy, but also from the Federal
Reserve through the banking system. Indeed, our economy
runs on credit. And if the Federal Reserve, the lender of last
resort, chooses to make more credit available, the economy
can grow. If it makes less credit available, growth will slow or
the economy may decline.

The Federal Reserve compiles another set of accounts
called the "Flow of Funds," or "Sources and Uses of Funds."
These data come closer than "saving" in the GNP accounts to
measuring and describing the kinds of financial transactions
we have in mind when we refer to financing business activity.

For 1988, our national income and product (GNP) accounts show gross saving of $642 billion, including Federal
government dis-saving of $146 billion. The Flow of Funds
statement, however, shows that $1,037 billion were raised in
the credit markets, $773 billion by the nonfinancial sectors.
The remaining $264 billion were raised and reloaned by the
financial intermediaries—banks and other financial institutions.

Even these large totals understate the amount of finance
available. They do not include, for example, trade and security credit or unpaid tax liabilities, as these are not sums
raised in the credit markets. Thus, when these economists
speak of the government absorbing private saving so we
cannot finance any growth, I can imagine a Mona Lisa smile
appearing on Mr. Greenspan's lips.

Finance is not a genuine limitation to economic growth in
this country. In 1983, with the economy just emerging from
recession, the lack of finance would have been an inexcusable
blunder. In 1989, tighter monetary policy was understandable, as the economy was near full employment and inflationary pressures were increasing. Labor compensation,
which was rising at a 4 percent rate at the beginning of 1988,
stepped up to a 5 percent pace by the end of 1989. Sure, Mr.
Greenspan is holding the monetary reins snugly. He should.

But the problem is not finance. The Federal Reserve can supply all the credit the economy can handle. What they and we would get for it, is less and less real growth, more and more inflation, and even greater inflationary expectations.

The problem is the lack of real resources—the kind that can be enlarged by more capital investment and productivity. There is nothing wrong with people's desire for pay increases and for a higher standard of living. At any time, some can obtain them at the expense of others. But we cannot all have more unless we produce it and raise total real incomes.

The Fed cannot help much in this direction. It can guide the economy along its existing growth track, laid out by fiscal policy. If we want a faster, sustainable track, fiscal policy will have to do it. That means two things: cutting government spending to free resources and providing the incentives to business to put these resources into investment and R&D. It isn't complicated. (I think it was Harry Truman who said, "Questions are simple; the answers are complicated." He knew economists, too.)

The end of the Cold War will provide a great opportunity for shifting resources out of government activities. Do not be disappointed, however, if budgetary savings do not appear overnight. It is expensive to redeploy troops, even to reduce forces, and to shut down bases. If the outbreak of peace is for real, count on two or three years before we begin to see significant cost reductions. Meanwhile, it is essential that Secretary Cheney, OMB, and the Congress monitor new appropriations and military contracts very carefully. Otherwise, it will take longer than two or three years.

Lie Two: "We're dependent on foreign capital." Certainly, foreigners found the United States an attractive place to invest money. A strong economy and a high cost of capital, among other factors, attracted enough foreign investment to bid up the dollar by 50 percent from 1980 to 1985. The result was a record trade deficit. That meant some of our companies going out of business, some going abroad to produce their products, and many riding out the storm here despite the large volume of lost business. Such is our "dependence" on foreign capital.

Mac Baldrige, the late Secretary of Commerce, once told me that "the trouble with most economists is that they have never been on the floor of a factory." If they had seen first-hand the "blessings" of the soaring dollar, maybe they would not speak of our dependence on foreign capital. Frankly, I doubt it. Faced with that choice, they would believe their theories and not their eyes. But they cannot escape the fact that the net inflow of capital is our trade deficit. This relationship is not just definitional, as in saving equals investment. It is also operational. Foreigners do not print dollars or create dollar reserves and deposits—the Federal Reserve System does that. So, as a group, they obtained their net accumulation of dollar assets by selling us more goods than they bought from us. It would be just as accurate and meaningful to say that we are dependent on our trade deficit. At least that is clearer.

As our trade deficit shrinks, and production therefore moves back to the United States, it will be interesting to hear the explanations of how we grew despite the loss of the net capital inflow. The irony may be that we will encounter some difficulty getting back to balanced trade. Near full employment, we cannot increase production rapidly for export and for domestic use. The "peace dividend" may help to provide some productive resources from defense manufacturers; and, of course, so would investment in additional facilities.

Some economists speak of foreigners financing our budget deficits and providing up to half of our domestic investment. That comes to a large part of the economy. Here, too, we are mixing finance with saving from the GNP accounts. The Federal Reserve Flow of Funds accounts provide a more accurate view of the foreign share. In 1988, foreigners supplied $112 billion to the credit markets, out of a total of $1,037 billion raised by all sectors and $773 billion raised by nonfinancial sectors. Thus, depending on which total is used, they supplied either 10 percent or 14 percent. But since both aggregates understate the total amount of resources, foreigners supplied somewhat less than those percentages. That hardly makes us foreign capital "junkies."

Furthermore, when we add that this capital inflow depresses our economy through our trade deficit, it is clear that

Mr. Morita and company are doing us no favor. They benefit from their investments here. The Brookings-Boston Axis also are warning us of the disastrous consequences of a shrinking capital inflow. What is their angle? Maybe it is just that they have never been on a factory floor.

Lie Three: "We're the world's largest debtor." Is it a sign of our weakness if foreigners invest here? No. If foreigners build factories here, does that make us a debtor? No. The United States government has not borrowed large sums in foreign currencies from foreign countries to enable us to import goods that we need as Mexico, Brazil, and other debtors have done. Foreigners are buying assets here because they find them attractive. In effect, they are participating in our economy.

That participation already has depressed our economy. The interest and dividends foreigners earn on assets they own are already out of our domestic income stream and will not detract further from our incomes. Note that GNP $= C + I + G + X - M$. That is, GNP—everything we produce—is equal to consumption plus investment plus government purchases plus exports minus imports. Imports are subtracted because those are goods and services we consume that are not produced here. They include payments of interest and dividends to foreigners because those payments represent our purchases of services from them.

The payments reflect the amount of assets foreigners already own here. Nearly all income generated by further growth in our economy will belong to us. Foreigners will increase their *income* here, net of our income from abroad, only as long as they increase their *investment position* here relative to our investment abroad. That will continue as long as our current account (mainly our merchandise trade balance) is in deficit. Therefore, either from the perspective of business output or income, we will benefit from the elimination of our trade deficit and its associated net inflow of capital.

In the spring of 1987, the administration—in this case, the Treasury Department—was considering issuing some of its securities denominated in yen. It was not for the purpose of financing projects in the United States or simply paying for imports. Japanese producers were happy to take our payments in dollars, as they still are. There were two reasons indicated for borrowing yen. One was to sell them to support the dollar, which was declining. The other was to reduce Treasury borrowing costs, because interest rates were—and still are—lower in Japan than they are here.

I argued against it for several reasons. Fortunately, others argued against it, too. Reducing interest cost that way could be very costly. The market price of the yen nearly doubled relative to the dollar during the preceding 10 years. While it may not rise as fast in the future, further increases are likely. I do not believe that the U.S. Treasury should be in the business of speculating in foreign exchange. We do not need a larger budget deficit.

A few people, inside and outside the administration, also suggested that borrowing yen would stabilize the foreign exchange markets, because we would be indicating our serious intent to support the dollar. I think it would have had the opposite effect. The markets probably would regard our borrowing yen as a sign of weakness. The most important reason not to borrow yen to support the dollar is that it would perpetuate our trade deficit, especially with Japan. Foreigners became interested in stabilizing the foreign exchange markets only after the dollar began to decline. I do not remember any interest on their part, or on ours either for that matter, in stabilizing exchange rates while the dollar was going through the roof.

I want to be careful that I do not create the impression that the dollar is our only problem or that it can provide the solution to our problems. It is not, and it cannot. Our policy toward the dollar should be to hold it down to levels that maintain our price competitiveness in the products we trade in world markets. In particular, the dollar should be lower than 144 yen. In 1988, U.S. hourly compensation for manufacturing production workers was about 10 percent higher than for Japanese workers. That was at an average dollar price of 128 yen. It is likely that U.S. productivity is still higher on average than in Japan, but I doubt it is higher in trade-sensitive industries like automobiles and electronics.

If our relative position in labor costs is similar in 1990 to what it was in 1988, the dollar should be at about 115 yen—possibly less to offset Japanese import restrictions and our disadvantages in quality and style. Certainly, we should not try to fix a particular rate in advance. That is probably impossible to do anyway. Our goal should be to eliminate our deficit with Japan, plus or minus a few billion dollars, by the mid-1990s.

Mr. Morita and company suggest that if we pressure them this way, they may pick up their marbles and play somewhere else. When we get our trade with Japan close to balance, we will find that it is all right. It will be clearer, then, that they have been playing here with *our* marbles all along. Reducing the trade deficit will add some business activity, especially in manufacturing; but a lower dollar also means higher import prices and more inflation. Furthermore, starting near full employment, if we do not add to our industrial capacity and productivity growth, increased export business will partly displace activity in other areas of our economy. More export business and orders may induce more fixed investment in manufacturing. However, I think the additional investment—with no further inducements—will be marginal, especially if a declining dollar raises inflation and interest rates.

Rising inflationary pressures in 1988 and 1989 prompted the Federal Reserve to tighten credit conditions. Economic growth slowed markedly in 1989. Through the year, analysts debated whether the economy would achieve a soft landing or hard one. With regard to our fundamental competitiveness and longer-term prospects, the debate was irrelevant. The economy can no longer sustain the 4 percent plus growth rate of the 1982 to 1988 expansion. The yellow brick road the economy was traveling ended before it reached the Emerald City of Oz. From here on, the economy is on a rocky road to nowhere special.

Probably all we can reasonably anticipate for the next few years is about 2.5 percent or so average growth per year—possibly a little more in manufacturing, according to charts 6–2 and 6–3. Beyond that much growth, inflation would accelerate and, sooner or later, end the expansion. Current actual growth and the economy's very sluggish leading indicators do not promise anything more.

One thing that could help, of course, is increased capital spending. But those prospects are not promising, either. During 1989, the Federal Reserve succeeded in holding the line on inflation at about 4 percent. At the same time, unit labor costs for all nonfinancial corporations accelerated to about a 5 percent rate.[1] The result was a squeeze on profit margins, and corporate operating profits fell about 10 percent from the third quarter of 1988 to the third quarter of 1989.[2] With slower growth in business activity, corporate operating rates eased from over 84 percent to about 83 percent.

The Federal Reserve's Flow of Funds statement shows that cash flow for nonfinancial corporations was running $50 billion below capital expenditures in 1989. That shortfall had worsened from $25 billion in 1988 and $19 billion in 1987 and must be financed externally at our relatively high capital costs. In 1984, the shortfall was also about $50 billion. But then we were rebounding from recession, the economy was booming, not sagging, profits were growing, and the investment incentives were in place.

Present conditions suggest that investment will slow, not accelerate. If we permit that to happen, we will tighten our grip on last place in world competitiveness. As Casey Stengel asked, "Isn't there anyone here who knows how to play this game?" If the answer is to raise taxes, whose would we raise? Undoubtedly, Congress will rally behind its usual battle cry of "equity" and "fairness." But at this stage of affairs, hitting the corporations again would be madness, not policy—which is no guarantee that it will not happen. Washington has well earned its reputation as the only insane asylum in the world run by its own inmates.

In March 1989, just before I left office, John M. Berry, the *Washington Post's* eminent columnist, wrote a "farewell article," which afforded me the opportunity to propose some

---

[1] Bureau of Labor Statistics, *Productivity and Costs,* USDL 89-580, December 6, 1989.

[2] Bureau of Economic Analysis, *Gross National Product and Corporate Profits, Third Quarter 1989,* BEA-89-51, November 29, 1989.

economic priorities or goals for the 1990s.[3] Nearly a year later, I would list the same ones, in the same order—a consistency, at least in this instance, that is not bad for an economist.

Priority One: Bring down inflation. It should not be first but, unfortunately, it has to be. If our inflation rate now were 1 or 2 percent, I would probably put it last and suggest that we aim to keep it that level. But underlying inflationary pressures are already moving above a 5 percent rate. A renewed wage-price-interest rate spiral would lead to stagflation again at best, or a severe recession at worst. "If I may use a football analogy, we need a solid defense. If we let inflation get out of control, we are going to get blown out of the game before we have a chance to move the ball."[4] (Actually, I am partial to baseball, but I thought I should spread the largess around a little.)

Mr. Greenspan's recent comment that he would like to eliminate inflation in the next few years is commendable, but for practical purposes unachievable. Pay increases, now running 5 percent or so, are locked in under contract for two or three years. To eliminate inflation within a few years or even five, would require a near-depression to accomplish— something neither private citizens nor government officials would tolerate. It probably would mean the end of the Federal Reserve's independence. Politicizing the Fed by putting it under the direct control of the Congress or the White House would be worse in the long run than our present inflation.

It is worth trying, however, and probably achievable, to cut inflation in half by 1995. However, that means maintaining slow growth from here on, certainly no faster than our gains in productivity. The wage-price spiral that is threatening to break loose is the economy's version of a dog chasing its own tail. The faster the spiral, the less progress we will make in any productive direction.

---

[3]John M. Berry, "The World According to Ortner," *Washington Post,* March 5, 1989, p. H1.
[4]Ibid.

My reference to some pickup in wage increases is not a criticism of our workers. There is nothing wrong with aspiring to rising standards of living. After all, the members of Congress just voted themselves a 40 percent increase in pay. They agreed, on the House side at least, to give up their honoraria for speeches. What it comes down to, as the comedian Jay Leno explained, is that "we'll have to pay them to shut up." Five percent increases for our *real* workers is not an unreasonable aspiration. The problem is that they cannot all enjoy that large a gain in living standards, because part or most of that wage increase will sooner or later be offset by price increases. Can they achieve 5 percent gains in real earnings? Certainly. How? By increasing the gains in productivity to 5 percent. That would offset the wage increases and permit employers to maintain stable prices.

Thus, Priority Two must be: Increase business capital spending. How do we do that if we are already near full employment? By Priority Three, the need to: Reduce the federal government's consumption of goods and services. That is, shrink the size of government direct purchases of goods and services. With much more progress toward world peace since early 1989, I am even more confident that we can free up the resources we need for large increases in capital investment.

Priority Four? Cut the trade deficit. Bring home all that business we lost during most of the last decade. You will see, we do not need their capital. We will enjoy playing with our own marbles for a change and maybe some of theirs as well.

Priority Five: Cut the budget deficit by bringing spending down. This will make those people who worry about the deficit feel better, and it will help to lower capital costs.

There are, of course, a number of other critical problems we must deal with to improve the quality of life in America. Problems involving the environment, drugs, crime, disease and health care, domestic violence, and the quality of everything we produce from education to cars. I have no special expertise in these areas and will not presume to offer detailed solutions for them.

But the "experts" do not seem to be making much progress either. Perhaps we need better laws to deal with some of these problems. In some cases, we do not enforce existing laws with sufficient determination. To deal with some problems, we need better organization. Rewards should accompany results more closely, as Mr. Gorbachev and Mr. Iacocca have discovered. Mr. Gorbachev seems to be doing something about it.

Nearly all of these problems require, or would benefit from, more resources. Therefore, they would appear to compete with the priorities I listed earlier. That may initially be true, to a limited extent. But in the longer run, they are complementary. Improved education can help to deal with all these problems. It can also add to productivity and thereby add to the economic benefits of increased capital spending. The increased capital spending will make more resources available in the future to deal with these problems. Meanwhile, the economic and social issues can run on parallel tracks. But even if we tried to integrate them into a single list, I would still leave capital investment at the top and the budget deficit at the bottom.

If we raised investment enough to lift the economy to a faster growth path, that alone would lower the deficit. Critics scoff whenever the White House talks about growing our way out of the deficit. The critics are right. We cannot accomplish this at a 2.5 percent rate of growth. At a 4 to 5 percent sustained growth rate, we probably could.

Faster growth would take care of another issue we are hearing more and more about. That is our ability to provide for social security pensioners in the future. Currently, we have five people of working age, 20 to 64 years, for each person 65 years of age or older. With an aging population structure, by the year 2020, we will have three workers to provide for each pensioner. The ratio will continue to decline gradually to two and one half-to-one in the year 2050. These are Census Bureau "middle series" projections based on current rates of fertility, mortality, and net migration. If the fertility and mortality rates decline, this ratio will come down somewhat faster.

How can we handle that? Easily, if worker productivity continues to improve. At 2.5 percent growth, productivity will double in 28 years. That is, before the year 2020. At 5 percent growth, it would double every 14 years, so that in the year 2023, *one* worker would produce as much as *five* workers do in 1990. Thus, if we have a problem at all, it is in promoting productivity and not in providing for our pensioners. We should stop worrying our elder citizens about it.

There are some policy measures we need to take to move the economy in the direction of the important priorities. The first is to maintain moderate expansion of money and credit, consistent with our capacity for real growth and the goal of reducing inflation gradually. Mr. Greenspan is doing a good job of it. Mr. President, may I suggest that you instruct your staff to leave Mr. Greenspan alone. Political interference can only lead to bad monetary policy, and it will be bad for the country in the long run.

Besides, our policy problems today are not monetary, they are fiscal. We need a genuine fiscal program. "Read my lips" and lowering the tax rate on capital gains will not cut it. Not even with the addition of Mr. Brady's "Family Saving Account." That account would provide tax-free interest and dividends on savings of up to $5,000 per year, but it does not provide any tax deduction for the saving itself. The package stands no chance of moving us from the rocky road back to the yellow brick road.

No tax increase is fine. But that is only what we will *not* do. We need something *positive* to boost real investment. The capital gains rate will provide only a small boost, and virtually none if it is legislated as a temporary measure. Nor will the Family Saving Account add materially to genuine national saving; most funds simply will be transferred from prior savings—that is, from an existing account into a new tax-free account. In the end, the lower capital gains rate and Family Saving Account will turn out to be little more than subsidies for Wall Street.

We need to reinstate the investment and R&D tax credits as they existed up to 1986 and do it quickly. In addition to these incentives, our tax system is in need of overhaul. The Tax Reform Act of 1986 did not do the job. One obstacle that seems always to be in the way of achieving an efficient tax system is an endless and even soul-searching argument over how "progressive" our tax structure should be. Somehow, we have to rid ourselves of this "guilt trip."

Our income tax structure was made steeply progressive in World War II. It was a wartime necessity that has remained part of the nation's tax system ever since. Its justification is political and social; it does not have a solid foundation in economic theory. In an outstanding survey of the literature on this subject, Walter Blum and Harry Kalven concluded that the case for progressive taxation was "uneasy."[5]

The one unwavering source of support for progressive rates has come from communist and socialist writers. A system of central planning does not need individual freedom and initiative.[6] Arthur Okun observed that in *The Communist Manifesto,* Marx and Engels put progressive income tax rates second to abolition of private land ownership. But in our tax system, it takes "center ring in the redistributive arena."[7]

Nonetheless, Okun strongly supported progressive rates. His justification was not in theory or analysis, but in a comment of Henry Simons that income inequality is "unlovely." But what the devil does that mean? Should an unskilled, illiterate worker be given the same net income as a skilled physician? (As a "skilled economist" or "skilled attorney," maybe. Are these oxymorons?) Should an average minor league baseball player be handed the same salary as a major league star? If the owner of a major league team voluntarily pays a star player $2 million to $3 million per year, should it be confiscated by the government because someone else thinks it "unlovely?" Is this a basis for rational economic policy?

Blum and Kalven provide a much better quotation from Lionel Robbins regarding high rates on upper incomes in England:

---

[5]Walter J. Blum and Harry Kalven, Jr., *The Uneasy Case for Progressive Taxation,* (Chicago: The University of Chicago Press, 1953).

[6]Ibid., p. 73.

[7]Arthur Okun, *Equality and Efficiency,* (Washington, D.C.: The Brookings Institution, 1975), p. 101.

They were brought into existence at a time of crisis when they did not seem—and indeed were not—inappropriate to the needs of the situation. Now that the crisis has passed, they have continued to exist because those who rule over us have been afraid to challenge the purely demagogic arguments by which they are usually supported.[8]

And similarly, a passage written over a hundred years ago by McCulloch: "The moment you abandon . . . the cardinal principle of exacting from all individuals the same proportion of their income or their property, you are at sea without rudder or compass, and there is no amount of folly you may not commit."[9]

The economic case for progressive taxation derives from the notion of declining marginal utility of money, but the curve presented in textbooks is pure speculation. Economists cannot quantify theoretically or empirically the precise shape of the curve for an individual, or show how to compare precisely the differences in the utility of money between or among individuals.

There is general agreement, I believe, that higher-income individuals or households should pay more dollars in tax; that is accomplished by a flat tax rate. But beyond that, the argument is uneasy indeed. Perhaps the system of graduated rates has persisted so long because of the unfortunate use (or misuse) of the expression "progressive," which connotes moving ahead or advancing. Progressive rates certainly do not promote economic growth; and what is worse, they are detrimental to economic efficiency.

If we are going to maintain an income tax system, we should adopt a flat tax, which is what tax reform was supposed to be in the first place. Samuelson and Nordhaus provide excellent justification:

"It [the flat tax] would put thousands of tax lawyers out of business. [That alone is worth it.] The economy would become more efficient as people spend less time worrying about the

---

[8]Blum and Kalven, *The Uneasy Case,* p. XIX.
[9]Ibid., p. 45.

impact of their actions on taxes and more time worrying about production of aircraft and computers and generation of innovations.[10]

Winston Churchill once said, "The vice of capitalism is that it stands for the unequal sharing of blessings; whereas the virtue of socialism is that it stands for the equal sharing of misery." For those of you who are determined to maintain your guilt, I would point out that even with the flat tax, the system would remain "progressive" because of low-income exemptions and government large-scale transfer payments.

The time has come also to shift part of the tax system to a value-added tax (VAT) or a consumption tax. The government is already struggling with the problem of how to raise personal saving. The proposals so far, involving IRAs or IRA-type benefits, have not worked and hold little promise of success in the future. The reason that they are not working is that people can take advantage of them without new saving, and they are superimposed on a tax system that encourages consumption.

If we really want to raise saving (and I cannot help repeating that it must be done as an adjunct to the encouragement of investment), we will be more successful with a different tax structure. Shifting at least part of the base from income to consumption taxes would encourage people to work more and spend less. Then we can stop wasting time devising new IRAs or Family Saving Accounts that never work.

Washington usually gets its act together only in time of national emergency, and then it does so magnificently. Unfortunately, America's traveling a slow road to economic mediocrity is not an emergency. The wolf is not at the door, and we are not in any danger that Thomas Malthus's warning will come true. But we can do better than we are. Our citizens want better standards of living, and I know there are enough elected officials in Washington who sincerely care. We can turn our country into America, the economically beautiful. Why not go for it?

---

[10]Paul Samuelson and William D. Nordhaus, *Economics,* 13th ed. (New York: McGraw-Hill, 1989), p. 790.

In the course of presenting these arguments, I may have been a little too harsh on economics or economists. After all, one should not knock one's own profession. You should continue to listen to economists. They do have lots of ideas and sometimes good ones. And, as Will Rogers once said, "They're as likely to be right as anyone else."

INDEX